Trieste and the Meaning of Nowhere

T0182375

Trieste and the Meaning of Nowhere

JAN MORRIS

DA CAPO PRESS
A Member of the Perseus Books Group

Copyright © 2001 by Jan Morris
Map copyright © 2001 by Anita Karl and Jim Kemp

All rights reserved. No part of this publication may be reproduced, stored in a retrieval system, or transmitted, in any form or by any means, electronic, mechanical, photocopying, recording, or otherwise, without the prior written permission of the publisher.
Printed in the United States of America.

Cataloging-in-Publication data for this book is available from the Library of Congress.

ISBN-10: 0-306-81180-4 ISBN-13: 978-0-306-81180-7
First Da Capo Press edition 2002
Published by arrangement with Simon & Schuster.

From *The Collected Poems of Wallace Stevens* by Wallace Stevens, copyright 1954 by Wallace Stevens. Used by permission of Alfred A. Knopf, a division of Random House, Inc.

"Watching the Needleboats at San Sabba," from *Collected Poems* by James Joyce, copyright 1918 by B.W. Huebsch, Inc., 1927, 1936, by James Joyce, 1946 by Nora Joyce. Used by permission of Viking Penguin, a division of Penguin Putnam, Inc.

Published by Da Capo Press
A Member of the Perseus Books Group
http://www.dacapopress.com

Da Capo Press books are available at special discounts for bulk purchases in the U.S. by corporations, institutions, and other organizations. For more information, please contact the Special Markets Department at the Perseus Books Group, 11 Cambridge Center, Cambridge, MA 02142, or call (800) 255-1514 or (617) 252-5298, or e-mail j.mccrary@perseusbooks.com.

For

ELIZABETH

and in memory of

OTTO

9th Queen's Royal Lancers

Jan Morris lived and wrote as James Morris
until she completed
a change of sexual role
in 1972.

CONTENTS

I was the world in which I walked, and what I saw
Or heard or felt came not but from myself

Wallace Stevens

Munich
Danube R.
Linz
GERMANY
Salzburg
Innsbruck
AUSTRIA
Drau R.
Bolzano
JULIAN ALPS
FRIULI-
VENEZIA
GIULIA
LJUBLJ
ITALY
SLOVEN
Trieste
Venice
Gulf of
Venice
Opatija
ISTRA
Po R.
Pula
Adriatic
Sea
©H·Karl/J·Kemp, 2001

SLOVAKIA
VIENNA
Bratislava
Danube R.
BUDAPEST
HUNGARY
Trieste's
EUROPE
Drava R.
ZAGREB
CROATIA
Sava R.
BOSNIA & HERZEGOVINA
Kms
0
50
Miles
50

PROLOGUE

An Angel Passes

I cannot always see Trieste in my mind's eye. Who can? It is not one of your iconic cities, instantly visible in the memory or the imagination. It offers no unforgettable landmark, no universally familiar melody, no unmistakeable cuisine, hardly a single native name that everyone knows. It is a middle-sized, essentially middle-aged Italian seaport, ethnically ambivalent, historically confused, only intermittently prosperous, tucked away at the top right-hand corner of the Adriatic Sea, and so lacking the customary characteristics of Italy that in 1999 some 70 percent of Italians, so a poll claimed to discover, did not know it was in Italy at all.

There are moments in my life, nevertheless, when a suggestion of Trieste is summoned so exactly into my consciousness that wherever I am, I feel myself transported there. The sensation is rather like those arcane moments of hush that sometimes interrupt a perfectly ordinary conversation, and are said to signify the passing of an angel. Perhaps on Biblical grounds —something to do with the Crucifixion?—these are popularly supposed to happen at ten minutes before the hour, and it is odd how frequently they do.

For me they often signal Trieste. Ever since I arrived there as a young soldier at the end of the second world war, this city has curiously haunted me. Whatever has happened to Trieste, however much it changes, however often I go there, for more than half a century the feelings it stirs in me have remained the same, and in those moments of sudden stillness I am not simply re-visiting the place, I am re-examining myself too. When the clock stands at ten before the hour, and the unseen courier flutters over, I find myself all alone on the waterfront at Trieste, as it was long ago, and as it always remains for me.

The Adriatic is blue and silent, not a breath of wind stirring. Across the bay a small white castle stands, and the hills around are harsh. The sun blazes, but not radiantly. A desultory tug crosses the harbour; a train clanks somewhere; a small steamer belches smoke; a band plays in the distance and somebody whistles a snatch of Puccini—or is that me? The heavily pompous buildings that line the shore, spiked and pinnacled with symbolisms, seem to be deserted, as in siesta, and on the quay's edge a solitary angler sits hunched and motionless over a float that never bobs. Flags are listless. A tram waits for passengers. The same angelic interlude that visited me at home in Wales seems to have reached Trieste too.

None of my responses to these scenes are exuberant, but they are not despondent either. I am homesick, I am thinking sad thoughts about age, doubt and disillusion, but I am not unhappy. I feel there are good people around, and an unspecified yearning steals narcotically over me—what the Welsh language, in a well-loved word, calls *hiraeth*. Pathos is part of it, but in a lyrical form to which I am sentimentally susceptible, and at the same time I am excited by a suggestion of sensual desire. The allure of lost consequence and faded power is seducing me, the passing of time, the passing of friends, the scrapping of great ships! In sum I feel that this opaque seaport of my vision, so full of sweet melancholy, illustrates not just my adolescent emotions of the past, but my lifelong preoccupations too. The Trieste effect, I call it. It is as though I have been taken, for a brief sententious glimpse, out of time to nowhere.

I AM not the first to associate the city with nowhereness. The Viennese playwright Hermann Bahr, arriving there in 1909, said he felt as though he were suspended in unreality, as if he were "nowhere at all." Trieste is a highly subjective sort of place, and often inspires such fancies. People who have never been there generally don't know where it is. Visitors tend to leave it puzzled, and when they get home remember it with a vague sense of mystery, something they can't put a finger on. Those who know it better often seem to see it figuratively, not just as a city but as an idea of a city, and it appears to have a particular influence upon those of us with a weakness for allegory—that is to say, as the Austrian Robert Musil once put it, those of us who suppose everything to mean more than it has any honest claim to mean.

The very geographical situation of the city is suggestive. It always seems to be on a fold in the map, hemmed-in, hole-in-corner. A narrow coastal strip, never more than a few miles wide, is all that connects it with the body of Italy. For the rest it is closely enveloped by Slav territories: the frontier of Slovenia runs five miles from the city centre, Croatia begins ten miles to the south, Serbia, Bosnia-Herzegovina and Hungary are all within a day's drive. Trieste is like a peninsula settlement, on a spit protruding out of western Europe into the sea of the Balkans. "The last breath of civilization," thought Chateaubriand in 1806, "expires on this coast where barbarism starts."

Organically it is just as isolated. Close behind Trieste, pressing down towards the sea, stands an outcrop plateau of the Julian Alps. You must cross it to get almost anywhere, and the city stands confined between its slopes and the Adriatic. It is not a genial plateau, either. It is a loveless limestone formation from which geologists have evolved the generic name of karst. The Italians call it the Carso, the Slovenians the Kras, the Croats the Krs, and in all their languages the name is onomatopoeic: the Karst is tough, flinty, pot-hole country, sparsely vegetated and riddled with caverns and underground streams. The slopes immediately above Trieste have been softened by tree-planting, but the Karst was a forbidding obstacle for travellers in the days before good roads or railways, so stony and sterile was it, and infested by bandits. Even now it suggests to me a zone of quarantine or exclusion, the sort of region that is marked with hatching or dotted lines in historical atlases.

Sometimes it has been delineated in that way, too, because historically Trieste has been decidedly ambivalent. You *need* a historical atlas here. The place began as a coastal village of Illyrians, a hazy Indo-Celtic people who traded with their immediate neighbours in fish, salt, olive oil and wine. Rome colonized it, calling it Tergeste, Venice pestered, raided and sporadically occupied it, and at the end of the fourteenth century its local rulers entrusted it to the protection of the Habsburg monarchy in Vienna. This was the making of it, because four centuries later it was the Habsburgs who brought it into the modern world. They were then achieving peace at last with their ancient enemies the Turks, and having come to rule all that corner of the Adriatic determined to make their continental empire a maritime empire too. They chose Trieste to be its main sea-outlet to the world.

In 1719 they declared the city a Free Port, granting it many civic privileges and exemptions to encourage its development. They built a new town on its shore, and eventually they made it a great deep-sea port, in effect the port of Vienna. The merchants of Trieste became the real rulers of the place, superseding the remnants of its indigenous patriciate, robustly co-existing with the Habsburg bureaucracy, and surviving three brief periods of Napoleonic occupation. Connected to its hinterland to the north by roads and railways across the Karst, Trieste prospered mightily from the trade of Austria, Hungary, Bohemia and much of central Europe. By the turn of the twentieth century it was one of the world's great ports, a major point of connection between Europe and Asia. "The third entrance of the Suez Canal," they used to call it; the first commercial vessel to sail through the canal, even before its official opening, was the steamship *Primo* of Trieste, and three more were present at the inaugural ceremony in 1869.

So Trieste was an imperial creation, and for a few generations it was imperially satisfied. The bill of lading "Via Trieste" was familiar wherever merchant ships sailed. This heyday did not last long, though. In 1919, at the end of the first world war, the Habsburg empire fell apart. The newly invented kingdom of Yugoslavia inherited most of its Adriatic possessions, but Trieste found itself snatched from its geography, as it were, and appended to the recently united kingdom of Italy, whose easternmost outpost it became—on the frontier of barbarism, politicians in Rome doubtless still thought. It was deprived of its own interior. The port of empire inevitably withered, having no obvious purpose within Italy, and the city declined into torpor—as Pope said of Vestal Virgins, and Gibbon of Ethiopia, "the world forgetting, by the world forgot."

When in 1945 Italy in its turn was humiliated in the second world war, poor Trieste was bandied among the victors. The now Communist rulers of Yugoslavia coveted it, backed by their ideological comrades in the Soviet Union; the western Powers feared it might become a Russian outlet to the Mediterranean. For a time the place was divided between rival occupying armies—Britons and Americans in one part, Yugoslavs in another—and for a year or two it became an independent Free Territory under the auspices of the United Nations. But the antipathetic Powers of the Security Council, stymied by each others' vetos, could never agree upon an acceptable governor for it, and so under the pressures of the Cold War the Free Territory project was abandoned. In 1954 the port-city proper was handed back to Italy, and most of its immediate surroundings went to Yugoslavia.

Nearly half a century later the Yugoslav People's Federation disintegrated too, and so it is that today Trieste still hangs there at the end of its Italian umbilical, formally cut off from its hinterland—after those few glittering years of imperial celebrity, never yet fulfilled again.

FOR ME Trieste is an allegory of limbo, in the secular sense of an indefinable hiatus. My acquaintance with the city spans the whole of my adult life, but like my life it still gives me a waiting feeling, as if something big but unspecified is always about to happen. The streets of Trieste today are as traffic-jammed and noisy as any other European city of a quarter of a million souls, but they still strike me as half-empty even at their most crowded moments, and I feel alone there even when I am among friends. For nearly half a century the place has been part of Italy, and it is the capital both of its own eponymous province and of the much wider Friuli-Venezia Giulia region; yet to me it is still an enclave *sui generis,* where Latins, Slavs and Teutons have mingled, where artists, drop-outs, renegades, exiles and remittance-men can retreat and with luck be happy—like Browning's man-about-town Waring, who ran away from London to escape the world's weariness, and was last spotted with a laughing urchin on a Trieste bum-boat, hawking wine and tobacco to a passing English brig. And outsider that I am, I still see myself as part of that half-real, half-imagined seaport, so now that after all these years I am writing a book about Trieste (my last book, too) it is bound to be a work partly of civic impressionism, but partly of introspection—or self-indulgence.

"And trieste," wrote James Joyce of this city, "ah trieste ate I my liver." The phrase is apparently an adaptation of an Italian idiom about being ill-humoured, and also possibly a pun on the words *triste était mon livre:* but its subliminal hints—of the visceral, the surreal, the lonely, the hypochondriac, the self-centred and the affectionate—roughly approximate my own reactions.

ONE

A City Down the Hill

If you come to it by car over the Karst, all the same, Trieste looks perfectly self-explanatory. The road crosses the border out of Slovenia and reaches the village of Opicina, where the plateau abruptly falls away through pine-woods towards the sea. There, a tall obelisk marks the beginning of the city. It was erected in 1830 to commemorate the completion of the first proper highroad across the Karst, connecting Vienna with its seaport on the Adriatic. Now the monument is peeling and neglected, and its setting is suburban, but when it was new, it told the grateful traveller that his journey across the wasteland was over, and he was reaching a haven of imperial order—an up-to-date Mediterranean outpost of the empire of the Habsburgs. The young Austrian Archduke Ferdinand Joseph Maximilian came this way in 1850 and thought the Karst a cursed desert, but he saw the distant appearance of the obelisk as a symbol of hope, and urged his coachman to get a move on.

For me an element of hope is the essence of cityness, and when I see a city in the distance, out of the open country, I always get a move on myself. The more isolated the city, the more hopeful, because then it offers a more spectacular contrast to the bucolic world outside. Until lately the cycle of the country-side was regular and foreseeable, governed by the seasons and the primeval needs of agriculture: the harvests came and went, the lambs were born and slaughtered, sowing and reaping, calving and hay-making—day after day, year after year, the dutiful round proceeded. All being well, there were no surprises. Even the advent of silage and artificial fertilizers, even the prospect of genetic interference, has not yet freed rural living from its age-old routines. Winter or summer, rain or shine, sharp at six o'clock every morning of his life my neighbour Alwyn Parry drives up our lane in his pickup to prepare the cows for milking.

But the city! There matters change by the hour, and people too. The city bursts with ideas as with traffic, a swirl of newness and surprise. Who can be bored in a city? If you are tired of one activity you can try something else, change your job, take your custom to another restaurant. Most human progress has been engendered in cities. While the farmer ploughed his same old furrow, supervised by priest and landlord and succeeded when the time came by sons and grandsons, away in the city people were devising new ways of living, dressing, thinking, eating and believing. "Had I but plenty of money," the poet said (Browning again), "Money enough and to spare, / The house for me, no doubt, were a house in a city square. / Ah, such a life, such a life, as one leads at the window there!" I agree with him, life-long country-dweller though I am. In our own times urbanism has begun to overwhelm the rural way of things, but there is still enough disparity between town and country to make me prod my postilion when I see a city down the hill.

. . .

SURREAL? Hypochondriac? Subliminal? Surely not. Our first sight of Trieste from the Opicina obelisk, high on the ridge above the city limits, is as reassuring now as it was in Maximilian's time. The city sprawls before us apparently explicit and composed, and its setting is superb. If the weather is fine we can see it all, there and then, like a diagram of its history. Trieste lies around two bays, the bay of Trieste to the north, the bay of Muggia to the south, separated by a promontory—*The* Promontory, Triestini used to call it. The coastline stretches away towards Split and Croatia one way, towards Venice and Italy the other, with the blue hilly outline of Istria to the south, the flat shore of Friuli-Venezia Giulia to the north and west. Often this tremendous scene is blurred—by rain or fog in the winter, by heat-haze in the high summer—but sometimes it is almost preternaturally clear, and then one can fancy a flash of sunshine from the golden domes of San Marco in Venice, seventy miles away across the waters.

On a little hill below us, beside Trieste's northern bay, stands the original walled settlement of the city, known to the Illyrians, the Romans and the Venetians. It has a cathedral and a citadel upon its summit, a Roman amphitheatre in its flank, and its medieval tumble of streets is still recognizable, running down to the waterfront—the pattern of the small fortified port that grew out of Tergeste, and was perhaps rather like a less formidable Dubrovnik. Nowadays Trieste's Old City is partly obliterated by modern development, partly dingy with age, partly prettied up, and has lost most of its ancient pride; but beside and around it, overpowering its consequence, is the city the Habsburgs built as their imperial port.

The prospect of this other Trieste, much of it gleaming new

in Maximilian's day, must have cheered him up with its promise of white tablecloths and decent beds. This was a universal compensation of imperialism, and his contemporaries in British India found their spirits similarly rising when their trains drew into Bombay or Lahore out of the endless Indian plains. "See you at the Club!" they cried to each other in relief, as they hurried off to their hansom cabs, and Maximilian, after a look at the view from the Obelisk (which still gets a capital O in Trieste), doubtless hastened back to his carriage, shuffling the leaves from his boots, in the same expectant frame of mind. There in the lee of a wilderness Habsburg Trieste was built, in the eighteenth and nineteenth centuries, with all urban refinements. Its design was logical, its buildings were substantial, its streets were spacious, its manner was amply complacent, for it was a mercantile city, a port city, built for the job. It was not primarily concerned with politics, grace or leisure, like its architectural contemporaries St. Petersburg, Calcutta or Bath. Hard work and enterprise were its hallmarks, but its builders knew that creature comfort was next to profitability. It was a thoroughly modern and efficient urban machine.

Today both old and new Trieste are invested by industrial works and nondescript suburbs of the last century, but from Opicina an imaginative eye can still see their first relationship—an imperial relationship again, one settlement vastly dominating the other. The one is still cramped beneath its castle, vestigially walled: the other confidently faces the sea, with quays and jetties all along its waterfront, a grand splash of a piazza opening directly upon the Adriatic, and a lighthouse on a mole enclosing the harbour. The little medieval town has a certain delicacy to its muddle; the big Habsburg city has no subtlety, only measured swank. From one you might hear the music of lutes and madrigals, from the other oom-pah-pah. For a contemporary parallel you have only to go down the holiday coast into Croatia, where proud old Venetian cities are awash in concrete hotels and camping sites: but again the contrast would be familiar enough to officers of British India, because the complex alleys of castellan Trieste stand amidst the symmetry of the Austrian city rather like an Indian bazaar town beside a neat and whitewashed cantonment of the Raj.

Yet time and setting have made a unity of them (as they often have of the bazaar and the cantonment, and even of the camp-sites and the campaniles). At the start of the twenty-first century there are few modern structures down there, by the standards of most European cities. Trieste was not badly damaged by the wars, and high-rise buildings are rare—local guidebooks call a six-storey structure a *grattacielo,* a skyscraper. If we look selectively enough towards the city centre we still see much of what Maximilian saw, except that in his day the northern bay down there, the bay of Trieste, was massed with masts and riggings, and there were ships tied up at all those jetties, steamboats coming and going and wagons rumbling along cobbled piers. "All motion and animation," Maximilian thought it then. If a warship of the Imperial Navy sailed in she was greeted with a gun-salute from the castle, and a muffled echo would reach up here to the Obelisk itself.

Today that bay is more subdued. Farther away from us a new port has arisen, around the promontory in Muggia bay, and we can see tankers and container vessels moored there, or coming in and out: but immediately below us the central waterfront of Trieste, during a few grand generations the sea-gate of an empire, is likely to be without any ships at all.

FOR THE view from the Obelisk is hallucinatory, like our glimpse of Venice in the sunshine. Only for a century or so was Habsburg Trieste as assured as it looks from the hill. It was an *ad hoc* port, deliberately chosen and developed for imperial purposes, and ports are more vulnerable than most cities to the vagaries of history. Across the world we may see famous old havens now neglected or debased, sometimes simply because modern ships need deeper water or different facilities, but sometimes because their fundamental purpose has been lost. Everywhere once vigorous waterfront areas have been emasculated or mutated, with reconstituted flagstones and fancy fittings, warehouses turned into trendy apartments, novelty shops smelling of pot-pourri, dry docks filled in for more office space. The quays where the lovely clippers berthed in Manhattan now form a maritime museum. The docks in London where the East Indiamen unloaded their jutes and spices have been turned into Docklands, a grim modish city of corporations. Bristol and Liverpool, once great bases of the Atlantic trade, now find themselves on the wrong side of Britain for the European markets, just as one day Hong Kong may wish it were on the mainland of China after all. Nearly everywhere the jumble of port life, with all its stinks, noises and clashing colours, has been removed from city centres, and so from the public consciousness.

Much of this happened to Trieste too, abruptly before its

time. The port was not outmoded in any technical sense. It was simply made irrelevant by the collapse of the empire that created it, and it has never been the same again. Empires come and go, and their functions go with them. There may be a vessel or two down there—a warship perhaps, a car-ferry, a tug, a tourist hydrofoil—and we can see the usual conglomeration of yachts and launches in the inevitable city marina. But the bay of Trieste looks a regretful bay. It can never be what it was, and reminds us from the start, as I was first reminded half a century ago, that this city was built to a lost purpose.

Trieste awaits us notwithstanding. "Hurry up, coachman," Maximilian calls as his carriage pulls away from the Obelisk, "the Governor is expecting us for dinner." We ourselves just press the accelerator, remembering that we haven't got a hotel reservation. Whichever century we inhabit, down we go, down the hairpin bends from Opicina, our leather seats creaking or our plastic dashboards rattling, down from the Karst into the grey streets of Trieste (or Triest, as the Austrians spell it, or Trst as the Slovenes prefer, and the Croats down the road).

TWO

Preferring a Blur

We need not really hurry. His Excellency the Governor is of course honoured to receive the Archduke any time he arrives in the city, and we shall find that there are plenty of vacancies at the Albergo Ducha d'Aosta. Trieste can be a bewildering city, but it is habitually free of hassle. You can *drift* through this place, thinking about something else, as easily as anywhere in Europe. Its traffic generally stops for you at pedestrian crossings. Its buskers and beggars thank you politely if you give them something, and do not reproach you if you decline. Everyone seems pleased to be helpful.

It is not, mind you, a city made for pedants: the shop you want has probably adjourned for the holidays, the museum is temporarily closed for refurbishing, you've just missed the bus owing to schedule changes, the gallery is not in the telephone book and opens only in the summer season. But for the drifter it is just right. Even in the 1900s, when Trieste was in its powerful prime, it was a loitering kind of place. The English writer Robert Hitchens thought it half-asleep. Joyce liked walking about it, polishing phrases in his head. Italo Svevo wrote a novel largely concerned with strolling its streets, and the poet

Umberto Saba composed a lyric about wandering the entire city contemplating his own "grave evasive life"—my own practice exactly, except for the gravity.

SO OUR entry into Trieste is unlikely to be demanding. Since we have arrived in the evening (*vide* the Governor's dinner party) and on a day in the fall (*cf* Maximilian's shuffling of the leaves) the traffic is thick, but not frenzied. There is not much blasting of horns—road-rage is not a Trieste failing—or blowing of police-persons' whistles. When the street lights come on they are subdued, and at the end of an autumn day's work the city hardly feels as though it is preparing for an evening out, only ambling home to the game shows on TV.

It is hardly an inspiring introduction, either. The outskirts of the city are shabby, drab and colourless, the downtown centre is sombre. Statues, fountains and frescos are everywhere, but in the gathering dusk all seems monochrome. Heavy arcaded streets lurch in parallel past our windows, with pompous palaces of plutocracy one after the other, a Gothically steepled church here, a stately railway station there. The General Post Office is enormous. The Banca d'Italia is immense. The Palace of Justice is foreboding. Steep stone staircases link one street with another. A tunnel inexplicably disappears into a hillside. What looks like a prison is only an old dock warehouse. What is surely the Prefect's Palace is a branch office of an insurance company. Paul Theroux, recording his impressions of Trieste in 1995, employed the adjectives *serious, gloomy, dull, solemn* and *lugubrious.* To me Trieste on an autumn evening suggests the work of those English Victorian painters who specialized in seaports at the end of the day, with pale gaslight shining on wet pavements, and pub windows dimly illuminated. Also at such twilight moments I find it easy to imagine a Trieste handed over to the authority of some now defunct People's Republic, as it so nearly was in 1945, to be re-created swart, suspicious and smelling of sausages.

But if after checking in at the hotel we stroll around the corner to a restaurant, we shall find it, on the contrary, comfortably bourgeois. No fragrance of offal here, only of mushrooms or vegetable soup. The furnishings are plush, the lights are not glaring, near the door there is a serving-wagon loaded with fish on ice. No more than a dozen customers, I would say, are at their victuals in this decorous retreat, and they all look like members of the upper middle classes, of a certain age: doctors and their wives, we may surmise, a few academics, a bookseller perhaps, a couple of cultivated businessmen. They all seem to know each other, swopping pleasantries across the tables and eyeing one another's dresses without embarrassment. They listen with attention to each other's conversations, they are careful not to notice when a rucksacked couple comes in wearing jeans and T-shirts, and they are all clearly well-known to the management. For that matter so am I, if this is, as I rather think it is, the same restaurant at whose table, in 1978, I wrote with vinous pleasure in the book I was reading "Am I really *paid* to do this?"

And yes, presently the proprietor, excusing himself from his conversation with the obvious Professor of Slav Linguistics eating alone at the corner table, comes over to greet me. "How are things?" I ask him. "Much the same," he tonelessly replies, sweeping a hand around his half-empty restaurant. "We are still happy."

HE WAS surely speaking only half in irony, because it always seems to me that despite its public disappointments down the years, privately this city is generally content. In the morning, when we go out for our first daylight drift through town, if the weather is friendly we shall find it far more benign than we did last night. Those overbearing structures do not seem so severe, when sunshine and shadow flicker through the arcades, and the mathematical street plans turn out to possess a certain elegance. Nobody could call Trieste a picturesque or exquisite city. It has no lovely city parks and few buildings that you feel you could pick up, to my mind a characteristic of great architecture—think of the Chrysler Building, or the Doge's Palace, or the Romanesque chapels of Spain! When the sun shines, however, Trieste does have charm. As in all cities built to grid patterns, it can be difficult to know where you are, which way you are facing, whether the sea is this way or that: but often enough the wooded slopes of the Karst appear between the buildings, to set you more or less straight, or there is a glimpse of blue water across an intersection.

The city's first eighteenth-century planners built a neat pattern of streets around a short canal, the Canal Grande, which intruded into the city from the sea and was to provide safe moorings for sea-going ships, whatever the weather. This arrangement is still a pleasure to discover. The canal runs inland for a few hundred yards from the bay, and it is only about thirty feet wide, but handsome Neo-classical buildings line it, and at the end there stands a domed church, with Ionic columns in a grand portico, which gives a touch of ceremony to the ensemble. The canal is full of small boats, some of them half-submerged, a few actually sunk, almost all needing a lick of paint; three or four of the most derelict, hauled out of the water at the entrance to the canal, have been so splashed with vivid paints and graffiti, and are disposed so gracefully there, that they look like works of contemporary art. The canal quays are lively enough, if a bit shabby, and half-way up there is an outdoor market in a square, with mounds of fruit and vegetables, racks of dresses, flowers, socks and Mars bars.

Not too bad, you may think, your spirits rising rather. It is true that later architectural developments are less jolly even in the daylight—piles of nineteenth-century commerce, arid exercises in twentieth-century monumentalism—but there are many cheerful incidentals and exceptions. Perambulating central Trieste may not be exhilarating, but it is seldom dull. The lumpish offices of the city's boom days are still comically resplendent, inside and out, with allegorical images of aspiration and success. The private houses of long-dead bankers or shipowners, Gothic, Neo-classic or defiantly eclectic, stand on advantageous corners in glorious grandiloquence. Exercises in Art Nouveau, called here the Liberty Style, display gigantic bare-busted ladies guarding doorways or precariously ornamenting ledges. What's this, now? A Roman amphitheatre. Who's that? Verdi, composing, on a plinth in a garden. Which way are we going? Search me.

It is easy to get away from it all, anyway. Take a lane into *città vecchia,* the Old City, clamber up its steep slope through a minuscule piazza, like a village square with groceries and bric-a-brac stores in it, skirt a Roman archway and a couple of churches, and soon we shall find ourselves on the flat summit of St. Giusto's hillock, where the citadel is, and the cathedral. This was the original city centre, but for the moment it need not, as the old Baedekers used to say, long detain us. As a whole it has a laboured institutional air. The Romans built their forum up here, and there are a few carefully repositioned columns around, together with war memorials, cemeteries, gardens of remembrance, a collection of armour, a lapidary museum and other such municipal essentials. Still, the air is fresh and the views are fine: and when we have seen enough, and taken a cup of coffee at one of the outdoor stalls in the cathedral piazza, it is agreeable to wander down again, past the hillside villas, past the Roman arch, through the quiet little square, past the junk shops into the working streets below.

I PREFER a civic blur to a sight-seeing tour, which is why we have meandered the town in this throw-away manner. Fortunately for me Trieste has few formal sights to see. "The average traveller," Cook's Handbook pronounced in 1925, "would not make a point of staying long in Trieste," and in 1999 an American magazine writer advised that after five days "you've done the place." Again no need to hurry, then. When we feel like a long light lunch we can potter down to the Piazza dell'Unità d'Italia, the Piazza Unità for short, the eye of the city and the lingering spot par excellence.

It is more festive than most of Trieste. On its western side it opens directly on to the sea, and it is said to be the largest square in Italy. The big buildings surrounding it are splendidly self-satisfied ("rather showy, but imposing," allowed Cook's Handbook). Flags fly from the former Governor's Palace. Bold masonry allegories look down from the immense old headquarters of the greatest of all Trieste institutions, the shipping line Lloyd Triestino (*nata* Lloyd Adriatico). Our hotel over the way there flies the Italian flag too, and flaunts the proud date MDCCCLXXIII—near the prime of the place. The long mock-Gothic structure with the clock tower is the Municipality (Michez and Jachez, the two bronze Moors on the top, strike all the twenty-four hours), and here we are ourselves sitting at a table outside the Caffè degli Specchi, the Café of the Mirrors, which has been comforting its customers with coffees, wines and toasted sandwiches since the days of the Emperors.

In the autumn the square is not often crowded, but now that the day has warmed up it has a homely cheerfulness to it. Some emperor or other stands upon a column, pointing peremptorily towards the sea. What looks like a pile of rubble is really a Fountain of the Four Continents, celebrating Trieste's profitable connections with the world at large, and equipped with sculpted bales of commerce, like the opium crates that used to appear upon the crest of that other merchant metropolis, Hong Kong. Two tall bronze flagstaffs await a more significant day of the calendar to fly their ensigns. Here and there around the piazza small boys are kicking a ball about, and little girls daintily promenade with toy prams, occasionally peering in a stagy way at the dolls inside, and proudly watched by gossiping mothers at the café tables.

Ah, such a life, such a life, as one leads at the café there! We stretch ourselves and have another coffee—"the coffee of Trieste," the waiter assures us approvingly, as though to compliment us on our taste, "is the supreme coffee in the world." And when we pay our bill and wander off again, in half a minute we are at the water's edge. The Greek car-ferry moored along the quay sounds its deep siren—it's ten to four, and it sails upon the hour—and instantly time seems in abeyance. The shouts of the infant footballers are lost, and the wide bay extends before us like a sea of eternity. A tug churns its leisurely way from one pier to another. A solitary man sits over a float that never bobs. And look—remember?—across the water a small white castle stands, all alone, like a castle in a trance.

THREE

Remembering Empires

Maximilian would know that castle. He built it, and called it Miramar. He was the younger brother of Franz Joseph I, Emperor of Austria, Apostolic King of Hungary, King of Bohemia, King of Jerusalem, Prince of Transylvania, Grand Duke of Tuscany and of Cracow, Duke of Lorraine, Lord of Trieste, and he was a sailor by profession. Not long after our encounter with him at the Obelisk he became the commander of the Austrian fleet, with his headquarters in Trieste. The story goes that caught in a storm in the bay one day he took shelter in an inlet a few miles north of the city, and so fell in love with the setting that when he married Carlotta, daughter of the King of Belgium, he built them this pretty folly on the spot.

In a way it was a little like a romantic idealization of the empire itself, a fairy-tale mock fortress on this southern shore, and when I see it out there I am reminded poignantly of the passing of all empires, those seductive illusions of permanence, those monuments of hubris which have sometimes been all evil, but have sometimes had much good to them. In particular of course I am reminded of the Pax Britannica, which has been part of my life always, in fact as in imagination, and which originally brought me to Trieste—when I first came here a Union Jack flew in the Piazza Unità and British warships often lay at the quays ("They never seem to keep still," I heard an elderly Triestino say to his companion, one listless August day, as they watched the Royal Navy incessantly scrubbing its decks and polishing its brasswork . . .). The city was very poor then, in the aftermath of war, and I remember still as an imperial gesture the decision of a fellow officer of mine, as we sat together in a restaurant, to send some quite large sum of money, a few million lire in the nonsensical currency of the day, to two abject beggar-boys mouthing appeals outside our window—who pranced away down the street, delirious with delight, as if they had been rewarded by the King-Emperor George VI himself. Ours seemed to me a good empire then, and on the whole I think so still. Over the years I have learnt to look back at it only occasionally with shame (the fundamental principle of empire having soured on all of us) but more often with a mixture of pride, affection and pathos.

For most of its citizenry the immense Habsburg dominion, too, was undoubtedly a happy enough construction—not for its subversive idealists, the nationalists and social reformers who found themselves ruthlessly suppressed, but for ordinary people who simply wanted to live in secure contentment. It was an autonomy of the stuffiest kind, but like Miramar it had charisma—the saving gift of grace. Its pomposity could be endearingly comical, and it had a gift for *Fortwursteln,* what the English called muddling through, which tempered its absurd obsessions about rules, ranks, regulations and forms of etiquette. Besides, in its apogee, which was also the apogee of Trieste, it did not work badly. Slow and laboured its methods might have been, but they gave people a comforting faith in the underlying competence and benevolence of Authority, however distant: and Authority itself, Authority almost in the abstract, was personified in the diligent figure of the Emperor, Franz Joseph the Father of his People, who went to his office in Vienna scrupulously at eight each morning, wore only a simple military uniform and preferred boiled beef and sauerkraut for his lunch. Many a simple citizen of Trieste doubtless thought of the imperial government, as did Joseph Roth's character Andreas Pum, that it was like something in the sky—great, omnipotent, unknowable and mysterious. "Though it was a delusion that our fathers served," wrote Stefan Zweig of his childhood's empire, "it was a wonderful and noble delusion. . . ."

At one time or another the Habsburgs had ruled many parts of the world, but their Austrian empire had no overseas possessions, despite the Emperor's hypothetical kingship in the Holy Land. This empire thought of itself as embracing rather than commanding, of assimilating all its scores of constituent peoples into one imperial family—the lesser nations were nations no more, but "provinces." The empire's only shoreline was on the Adriatic, and traditionally the Austrian fleet was no more than a theoretical factor in the balance of Europe. This made Miramar even more a paradigm: the little castle stood there with a toe in the world's ocean, fancifully.

Trieste was one of the great achievements of Habsburg imperialism. Although it had been under their protection since 1382, the Austrians had shown little interest in the place until in 1719 Charles VI declared it a Free Port. It was his daughter Maria Theresa who caused the Canal Grande to be excavated, and presided over the construction of a brand-new town, still known as the *borgo teresiano,* the Theresian Quarter. This is the urbane development that cheered us up on our walk the other morning. It was designed by ardent graduates of the Academy of Graphic Arts in Vienna, who set out to create something fresh—a merchant city that was also a garden city, full of greenery and fountains, while obeying careful imperial laws concerning sanitation, safety and proportions. They filled in a mass of ancient salt-pans to do it, and they built the Theresian Quarter in a modestly elegant Neo-classical style, with touches of Baroque. It consists of some fifty rectangular blocks, plus the canal and a couple of squares, and the merchants who occupied most of the houses had warehouses on the ground floor, offices and family quarters above. At the same time new piers were built on the harbour front, a lighthouse was erected and a new lazaretto—all such handsome and expensive works that half a century later Napoleon, himself no niggard when it came to display, scoffed at their extravagance. All of a sudden Trieste became a proper port, equipped for ocean traffic.

At first it was essentially an emporium, a market-place where goods brought by land or sea were assembled for sale, and then sent off again—a kind of permanent trade fair, with transport facilities. Before long the port had to be extended, and two new town quarters were built, rather less delicately: in Joseph II's time the *borgo giuseppino,* lapping at the walls of the Old City, and the *borgo franceschino,* named for Francis II, a little inland. All three quarters are still recognizable, and are known by their original names. But when in the 1850s the railways came down from Vienna, Trieste's functions shifted. It became instead a transit port, through which goods sold at source were passed to their buyers—Bohemian glass ordered from

Chicago, say, or Persian rugs destined for Munich. A whole *porto nuovo* was built, connecting with the railways on the northern side of the bay of Trieste. Now it is the *porto vecchio,* the Old Port, but then it was the very latest thing, and the Emperor himself came down to open it. Trieste entered its heyday. All the ancillaries of a port flourished—the agents, the financiers, the warehouse companies, the valuers, the ship repairers, the chandlers. Six banks and four great insurance companies dominated the city's finances, and the Chamber of Commerce became almost a government in itself.

Into this dynamic seaport poured a polyglot multitude. Some had been officially encouraged to take their varied skills there; others were simply drawn by the promise of the place, on the cusp between east and west, where you could make money almost as fast as you could in a California gold rush. Karl Marx, writing about Trieste in 1857, said that it was run by "a motley crew of speculators," Italian, German, English, French, Armenian and Jewish, which meant that it was not weighed down by tradition, and had the advantage, like the United States, of "not having any past."

DURING the reigns of six monarchs (Charles VI, acceded 1711, to Franz Joseph I, died 1916), the Habsburgs transformed a medieval fishing town into a modern international seaport, with a population that had grown from some 7,000 to 220,000. Perhaps the nearest equivalent is Hong Kong, founded by the British in 1840, and equally eruptive.

Hong Kong was Britain's declaration of intent in the Far East, and Trieste had a similarly symbolical meaning for the

Austro-Hungarian Empire. It was not just a great commercial asset; it also declared this vast continental sovereignty to be a maritime Power as well. Ever since they assumed responsibility for Trieste, in 1382, the Austrians had maintained a handful of warships in this corner of the Mediterranean, and used them in one conflict or another—to bombard fractious Venetians, to deter the French or help keep Turks at bay. After the Napoleonic wars they took control of the whole northern Adriatic coastline, and an Imperial Navy formally came into being, based at Venice. Its ships were given the prefix "SMS," for *Seiner Majestäts Schiff.* Its original professional style was British or German, but it grew to be thoroughly imperial, its ships Austrian-built, its officers Austrian gentlemen, its crews mostly Slavs.

When Venice was lost to the Austrians, in 1866, the fleet headquarters was moved to Trieste. This did not greatly please the merchants of the city, who thought it would leave the Venetians more time and space to rival them in commerce; nevertheless as a token of loyalty from the Chamber of Commerce they paid most of the cost of the fleet's first steam warship, the frigate *Radetzky,* and they fulsomely welcomed the Archduke Maximilian when he arrived in town to become the fleet's commander-in-chief. Very soon anyway the main base was moved again to the deeper and safer port of Pola, fifty miles away at the southern tip of the Istrian peninsula, but when the Imperial Navy wanted to put on a public show, with flags and manouevres before admiring grandees, inevitably it was in the bay of Trieste that its burnished ironclads assembled. When in 1866 the navy won a smashing victory over the Italians at the battle of Lissa, off the Dalmatian coast, no city in the entire empire, from the Turkish borders to the frontiers of Switzerland, celebrated more grandiloquently than Trieste.

By then Trieste occupied a special position in the Dual Monarchy (as the empire called itself when the Hungarians won their autonomy, and the ancient eagle of the Habsburgs acquired a second head). It was the chief port, whose water-gauge on the Canal Grande provided the zero point for all Austrian sea-charts. It was the capital of the Österreichischer Küstenland, the empire's one coastal province, embracing the whole of Istria and much of Dalmatia. And since 1850 it had been a *reichsunmittelbar Stadt,* a city owing direct allegiance to the Emperor himself. Anyone in the whole empire who wanted to travel overseas came down here to take ship. Businessmen Austrian, Czech or Hungarian conducted their foreign trade through the bankers and agents of Trieste. Soldiers and sailors were stationed here, actors and musicians came from Vienna to perform, holidaymakers and valetudinarians flocked to the lovely Istrian resorts. Franz Joseph, the nineteenth Habsburg to govern the destinies of Trieste, sometimes condescended to visit the place; as a reward for its loyalty to the Crown during the nationalist uprisings of the 1840s, it was officially dubbed *Urbs Fidelissima,* Most Faithful City.

THE MOST appealing aspect of the Austro-Hungarian Empire, at least in retrospect, was its European cosmopolitanism. It had few black, brown or yellow subjects, but it contained within itself half the peoples of Europe. It was multi-ethnic, multi-lingual, multi-faith, bound together only, whether willingly or unwillingly, by the imperial discipline. It was closer to the European Community of the twenty-first century than to the British Empire of the nineteenth, and possesses still, at least for romantics like me, a fragrant sense of might-have-been. Trieste was its true epitome. When they sang "The Emperor's Hymn," surely the most beautiful of all national anthems (better known to most of us as the melody of "Deutschland, Deutschland, Über Alles"), proud loyalists of Trieste sang it in at least three of the ten languages into which the lyric had been officially translated. Even in the city's imperial apogee, when it was known everywhere as an Austrian seaport, Trieste had a large Italian population, and its working language was Italian. Thousands of Slovenes and Croats had moved into town too, besides Marx's motley crew of adventurers.

The annals of nineteenth-century Trieste are full of foreigners who made themselves rich and eminent here. Remnants of the ancient local nobility still lived darkly in the Old City, where they variously claimed descent from the Romans or from a medieval guild of aristocrats called the Thirteen Families. They were, however, overwhelmed by the flamboyant invasion of aliens. How could they match, from their cavernous and crumbling palaces, the brilliant German Baron Karl Ludwig von Brück, a visionary local magnate and politico who proclaimed Trieste to be the open door of an immense fraternity of nationalities? Or the dazzling nouveau-riche Egyptian Antonio Cassis, nicknamed "Faraone," "Pharaoh"? The most lavish and prominent palazzo of the waterfront was built by the Greek shipowner Demetrio Carciotti, and the Englishman George Hepburn commissioned for himself a magnificent Palladian villa in the most commanding site on The Promontory. The limitlessly rich Morpurgos were Jewish. The Giustinette family was really Armenian. The American John Allen owned Trieste's first steamship.

Nevertheless standing as Trieste did so ambiguously between Latins, Slavs and Teutons, it was patently a city of Mitteleuropa. The merchant princes who ran it might be Italian, Slav or Jewish in origin, but like maharajahs in British India most of them shrewdly bowed to profitable imperatives, and were showily Austrian too. Sometimes they accepted Austrian titles; generally they lived in the Austrian style, florid and pompous but tempered by Biedermeier. It was natural that this cosmopolitan crowd should have contacts all over the world. When in 1817 the English piano-maker Thomas Broadwood wanted to present one of his instruments to his idol Beethoven, he shipped it to Trieste, where the local agents, who could arrange anything, had it sent on by horse and cart to Vienna. It is no surprise to learn that in 1909 the proprietor of a cinema in Trieste owned another in Bucharest and was presently to buy one in Dublin.

IMPERIAL Trieste was a well-ordered seaport. Streets were clean, crime was rare. Except at times of rebellious fervour, life was habitually calm. No gendarmerie could look much more reassuring than the officers of the municipal guard, called the *lamparetti* because of their nocturnal patrols, who glare back at us from their group photographs. They look a mature, stalwart, self-confident corps, more than a match for any hooligans or drunken seamen; all with virile moustaches, some with Franz Joseph whiskers too, wearing plumed Tyrolean hats and bearing themselves with tremendous authority (rather like the officers of the Monmouthshire Special Constabulary among whom my bearded maternal grandfather posed with equal firmness at about the same time). There was nothing provisional about the Imperial Government of Trieste. It was there to stay, and fine bodies of men were there to preserve it.

Trieste honoured all the forms of *K u K—Kaiserlich und Königlich,* Imperial and Royal. The Emperor's postage-stamp portrait, in a peaked military cap and a white tunic, hung in every tobacconist's shop, and beneath it was available the "chancery double," the prescribed sheet of paper upon which every official transaction or application, however trivial, must by law be written. Protocol was cherished and public parades were frequent—Franz Joseph believed frequent parading was a way of exorcising wars. There was a barracks with a huge parade square, instantly familiar to old sweats who had served their time on any of the empire's far-flung frontiers. Inspectors by the dozen supervised the quality of market food. Secret policemen tracked potential trouble-makers. An army of bureaucrats checked records, issued licences, ordered prosecutions, remitted discounts, inspected hygiene, regulated brothels, tabled statistics, sent reminders, received petitions, published decrees and sorted out problems of imperial etiquette. Trams, those emblematic mechanisms of Austro-Hungary, which trundled down the imperial streets in Serbia as in Poland, and were a part of the very ethos of Vienna—trams came early to Trieste, eventually even finding their way up the steep hill to Opicina and the Obelisk. Every house in the city was marked not only with a number, but with the name of its street too, with a single category of exception—and one can still hear some Undersecretary telling his clerk "But not, Ulrich, make it quite clear, not houses with subsidiary numbers like 41A, or 24B"—"Oh most certainly, Excellency, I shall see to that, most definitely not street names for houses with subsidiary numbers . . ."

Most citizens of Trieste were undoubtedly grateful for these benefits. They were grateful for the order of it all, for the safety of the streets and for the huge municipal hospital, occupying two whole city blocks in the most valuable part of town. They enjoyed themselves when the military bands played, the 87th Infantry Regiment drilled outside its barracks, or best of all when the Emperor himself ceremonially appeared, like a god from over the Karst, with infinite splendour of flags, feathers, gun-salutes and fireworks. They knew that theirs was more than just another city of the southern provinces, like Bozen, Agram or Laibach (one day to be transformed into Bolzano, Zagreb and Ljubljana). It was unique. Its style was set and its affairs were largely governed not by any languid local aristocracy, but by the Morpurgos, the Carciottis and the other powerful go-getters of the Chamber of Commerce. And the most important functionaries in town were not members of Ministries or armed forces, but of the Imperial Maritime Government, which had its headquarters in Trieste itself rather than in Vienna, in a charmingly pedimented waterfront building with white picket-boats on davits outside it.

This institution was the agent of the Dual Crown in everything to do with the sea, and it was very big in Trieste, where almost everything revolved in one way or another around the docks. It was a proud calling, to be a member of the Maritime Government or its ancillary the Trieste Port Authority. The Authority's grades of seniority were rigid, in the best imperial manner, and were emphasized for all to see by niceties of uniform: cocked hats for one grade, flat caps for another, dashing cloaks for senior functionaries, pilots' hats to have brims two and a half inches wide. Cap-badges, of course, displayed a gold two-headed eagle surmounted by the imperial crown, and outfits were supplied by the uniform-makers Guglielmo Beck and Sons of Vienna, who had a lucrative local branch.

WHEN the Italians took over Trieste, in 1919, even they admired the legacy of the Maritime Government, but long before then the empire had been losing its assurance, and Trieste had grown less and less the Most Faithful City. Musil satirized *K u K* in decline as the kingdom of Kakania, the kingdom of shit, and despite appearances by the turn of the twentieth century the whole grand structure was beginning to rot. Its methods were tangled in obfuscation, its protocols had become absurd, its armies were ineffective and Baron von Bruck's international fraternity was falling apart. It is the way of all empires, when they last too long. As their confidence shrivels and their apparently permanent convictions fade, they become caricatures of themselves. In my own empire the Victorian archetypes of lean frontiersmen or utterly incorruptible pro-consuls gave way in the end to silly old Colonel Blimp, with his walrus moustaches and his antediluvian ideas. In the empire of the Habsburgs the genial philosophy of muddling through degenerated into what Musil characterized as "the magic formula *Ass*," written at the bottom of almost every official memorandum and short for *Asserviert*—Awaiting Further Consideration.

No such prevarication had been necessary when, in the great days of the system, His Excellency had instantly determined that a 21A or a 42B did not merit a street name on its number-plate.

FOUR

Only the Band Plays On

K u K, all the same, never lost its spell over Trieste. Charles VI is that peremptory emperor on his column in the Piazza Unità. Leopold I holds his orb and sceptre above the Piazza Borsa and the Empress Elizabeth, "Sissy," Franz Joseph's wayward Bavarian wife, stands in the shade of the trees outside the railway station. Official buildings of the imperial prime still dominate many streets like so many mummified swells. Banks and insurance offices boast of old glories, with their marble and mahogany counters, their mosaic floors and their portentous statuary: within my own memory you had to bang a big silver bell with your hand to get attention in such a place, your cheque was authorized by rubber stamps with big wooden handles, and your money was discharged with a masterly hiss through a polished brass tube.

It is easy to enter the home of one of imperial Trieste's presiding grandees. It is a museum now, but a very personal one—a museum of him, really. Baron Pasquale Revoltella was an enormously rich bachelor, Venetian by origin, who had made his fortune by sometimes dubious speculations in grain, timber and meat. He spent a short time in jail, but worked his way back to respectability, and converted himself in later years into an archetypal tycoon of Franz Joseph's Trieste. He had a finger in a multitude of pies. He was a founder of the Assicurazioni Generale, one of the greatest of European insurance companies, and he owned the Hôtel de la Ville, the best in town. Most profitably of all, he was among the first to recognize the benefits of a canal through the Suez isthmus, eventually becoming the Austrian representative on the board of the Suez Canal Company, and its largest private shareholder. He had a villa in a suburban park, with its own chapel for his eventual burial, beside his mother; but it is his town house, designed for him by a German architect, that best expresses him, his vocation, his time and his city. Nowadays it overlooks the Piazza Venezia. When he built it the square was called Piazza Giuseppina, in honour of the Emperor Joseph II, and outside its windows was a statue of Rear-Admiral the Archduke Maximilian, late commander of the Imperial Navy, bald but bearded and in full uniform. Franz Joseph had been present at its unveiling, and the Baron was a prominent member of its sponsoring committee, which met inside his house.

Revoltella died in the 1870s and left his house to the city, stuffed with the works of art that testified to his culture and his wealth—"handsomely fitted up," commented Baedeker's *Austro-Hungary* approvingly in 1905. It has been enlarged in recent years to incorporate Trieste's civic gallery of modern art, but much of it is the same today as it was when he and his mother lived in it, an opulent hothouse of silks, velvets, chandeliers, tassels and gilts. It is not exactly Germanesque, it is not precisely Italian: it is in a mercantile high capitalist style that is very Triestine. Up its velvet-railed staircase, on one of Revoltella's grand reception nights, we imagine the *beau monde* of Trieste sweeping with their fans and sashes, some genuinely flattered to be invited to the house of the legendary nabob, some still loftily condescending.

Clutching the catalogue which the Baron has had printed for his guests, they inspect the wonders of his affluence. They marvel (or scoff) at the emblematic sculpture, half-way up the stairs, which is called *Cutting the Isthmus of Suez:* this has a plaque of Ferdinand de Lesseps on one side of its plinth, and a plaque of the Khedive Abbas of Egypt on the other, and is illuminated by a red electric bulb held between the wrought-iron fangs of a snake. They admire (or deplore) the specially commissioned painting, by Trieste's own master Cesare dell'Acqua, entitled *The Proclamation of the Free Port of Trieste* and tactfully honouring the origins of all this grandeur. They wonder how many of the leather-bound books in the library have actually been read, and how often anyone has sat at its purpose-built reading-chairs, with their folding bookrests, to consult Plutarch's *Life of Alexander.*

They are bemused, perhaps, by the plethora of commemorative coins, baronial crests, mementos of royal favour, images of Newton or Galileo and putatively panoramic views of the Suez Canal. They peer through the big telescope on its tripod, permanently aimed at ships in the harbour. They bow or curtsy to Signora Revoltella, who is too ancient to take part in the evening's festivities, but has been helped down from her bedroom to greet them. They sink gratefully into the soft red-plush chairs of the saloon, and even more gratefully at last into the dining-room, its immense table laden with crested silver, Bohemian glass and china from Bavaria.

Young Helga von Krantz whispers what a waste it seems, that the Baron should be a bachelor. Her husband the general growls that he's a lucky fellow. The Governor chats with his host over a large cigar, urging the benefits of preferential loading tariffs. Several gentlemen are huddled in a corner, deploring the effects of preferential loading tariffs. Several ladies tell the old Signora how much they admire her Modena lace collar, and she pretends to hear them. All is normal, all is stable, all feels as enduring as the empire itself. Still, a century and more later you and I may think the most revealing thing in Baron Revoltella's mansion is a small gilt-framed picture we spot in a corner: for when we look closer we find that it is not a picture at all, but a camera obscura set among the canvases, enabling the billionaire to keep an eye on the piazza outside, and make sure His Highness the Admiral is not vandalized on his pedestal by louts or nationalists. The Baron knows a thing or two, and does not have complete faith in those pompous old duffers the *lamparetti*.

THERE are many other places I like to go when I wish to sniff the imperial breezes. One is the railway station, southern terminal of the Sudbahn, which was the first of the lines connecting Vienna with Trieste. It is a building yellow, lofty and assured, in a mixture of classical and Renaissance modes that Habsburg Trieste particularly liked. Corinthian columns support its glass-panelled roof, sculpted women hold laurel-wreaths or engine-wheels, and there is any amount of floor-space for ceremonial welcomes. Silvio Benco, an eminent Trieste littérateur of the last *fin de siècle,* thought its architecture had "an athlete's poise, grace and nobility," and in his day, with its fashionable station restaurant and its hissing brass-bound locomotives, it must certainly have had confidence.

Then I like to wander around the old Central Hospital, in its day so generous an institution that poor mothers in labour were given a poverty payment—direct so to speak from the Emperor, like our donation from George VI. There is a quadrangle inside it, frequented by many cats squatting around a central image of the Virgin, and there I like to fancy the great medical men of old, taking a break in their pince-nez and white coats from the morning's consultations. Here comes Teofilo Koepl the obstetrician, deep in the latest paper on Caesarian parturitions from Vienna, and here is Arturo Menzel the chief surgeon tapping him on the shoulder to remind him about the staff meeting that evening, and importantly ignoring them both is Dr. Antonio Carlo Lorenzetti, who has no time to chat because, as everyone knows, he is also a member of the Governor's Council, not to mention being a Cavaliere of the Order of Franz Joseph. Patients lying on their beds in the sunshine respectfully watch them pass, and among the shrubberies the cats sit bolt upright, only their heads showing, like lemurs or prairie dogs.

The General Post Office of Trieste reminds me of the General Post Office in Sydney, Australia. Each is a telling memorial to its respective empire. Sydney's office is buried among skyscrapers, but holds its own by sheer Victorian assurance. Trieste's remains hugely dominant in a square of lesser institutions. Flags fly inside the Sydney building, and there are pictures of Queen Elizabeth II. In Trieste a stately carpeted staircase leads through a central salon to a bureaucratic maze of offices beyond. The post-boxes at Sydney are set in magnificent brass surrounds. At Trieste customers are provided with public lavatories and a bar. The sculptures on the outer wall at Sydney show contemporary postal services in action and were considered indecent when they were first unveiled. The presiding frescoes at Trieste present a female Mercury surrounded by happy cherubs playing cards. The Sydney General Post Office looks out on a Cenotaph, guarded by stone sentries with bowed heads. The Palazzo delle Poste in Trieste overlooks a mammoth fountain supported by tritons, their knees made green by the dripping of the water.

And there is always the Piazza Unità, the showpiece of the city then as now. There it is easy to summon back the high times of Trieste—1897, say, when Franz Joseph was about to celebrate the golden jubilee of his rule, and the city seemed to the world at large permanently fulfilled in style and function. The Piazza was rather a different place in those days. It was called simply the Piazza Grande, and a garden of trees almost filled its seaward side, between the palace of the Governor and the offices of Österreichischer Lloyd, Lloyd Austriaco. The premises of the Assicurazioni Generale occupied the Palazzo Stratti, above the Caffè degli Specchi, and on their parapet a benign female figure held a protective arm over a pillar, a human bust, a painter's palette and a railway engine, to represent Trieste guarding (for a proper premium) the interests of all the world. A tramline ran across the square, and now and then a No. 3 clanked along it. There was a bandstand in the garden; half-hidden by trees the liners of Austrian Lloyd tied up at the pier where the ferry from Greece ties up today.

Four cafés flourished in the piazza then, their summer tables almost meeting in the middle, and I prefer to hang out at the Flora, the most easy-going of them, frequented by journalists, poets, artists and such, dropping in from their homes in the Old City just out of sight. All around me first-class passengers, awaiting the time to board their ship, are enjoying their last half-hour on Austrian soil before sailing away to America, Alexandria or the east. There they sit at their tables in the sunshine, with their parasols and their ebony walking-sticks, greeting old acquaintances or introducing each other to fellow-passengers. Groups of friends fresh from Vienna or Budapest walk about the square, admiring the architecture, laughingly stepping back from the tram, the women holding up their skirts, the men often enough in the fancy uniforms of *K u K*. There are splashes of colour everywhere—braids and gilded epaulettes, bright silks of summer, gaudy parasols and pink fringed reticules. The music of a waltz sets people flirtatiously swaying as they chat: it sounds to me like something from Franz Lehár, and very likely is, since he is the handsomely pomaded bandmaster of the 87th Infantry who is conducting it in the bandstand.

Beyond the garden the harbour is alive. The big Lloyd liner has steam up: it's the new *Bohemia* sailing today, 4,380 tons, Trieste-built and famously luxurious, with double-headed eagles on all its drawing-room furniture, including the piano. Lesser traffic jostles around the piers. Vessels of the Hungarian-Croatian Line load up for Fiume and Spalato. Small steamboats with spindly funnels sail away to Grado, Venice or down the Istrian coast. Three-masters dry their sails in the roadsteads. Schooners from Greece or Sicily unload oranges or watermelons. Old black barges, with awnings and lines of washing, look like sampans in China, and Adriatic fishing-craft with red sails and blunt prows are painted with cabalistic symbols for luck. Sometimes a trader's launch or a pilot boat runs out to meet an incoming vessel ("A pilot for you to Trieste?" cried the cheeky boy on Waring's boat, but the master of that English brig had been here before—"the longshore thieves are laughing at us up their sleeves . . ."). Up the coast from the south comes a spanking warship, flying a huge imperial flag, and while the ladies at the cafés make a point of jumping in alarm when the saluting gun goes off from San Giusto, young Captain Lehár does not miss a beat.

Time to go aboard. A smart seaman in blue and white hastens around the square ringing a bell, and with handshakes and salutes gradually the crowd disperses towards the quay. A final sip of coffee (getting cold by now), a quick dash to retrieve that forgotten hatbox under the table, and the band speeds them on their way with a last lilting melody, the bandmaster bowing as he conducts when General von Krantz and his lady pass by. "Charming man," says she. "Humph," says the general.

THEY are only shadows, now, though, these vestiges of Habsburg Trieste, like so much in this crepuscular city. The great steam locomotives do not hiss in the station now, the Sudbahn station-master no longer welcomes important personages in his tight-buttoned livery; there is no express to Vienna any more, and when one day recently I went to see the morning train leave for Budapest I found it waiting rather pitifully at its platform—a diesel engine, two coaches, an uninviting dining car and only a handful of passengers at its windows. The mighty old hospital is still there indeed, but has long been superseded by a still mightier modern block on foothills behind the city. Only a solitary layabout was drinking in the bar of the General Post Office, when I last looked in. As for the scenes we shared in the Piazza Unità that day in 1897, I can hear the music still, but all the rest is phantom. The last passenger liner sailed long ago. The schooners, steamboats and barges have disappeared. No tram has crossed the piazza for years. The Caffè Flora changed its name to Nazionale when the opportunity arose, and is now defunct. The Governor's Palace is now only the Palace of the Prefect and the Lloyd Austriaco headquarters, having metamorphosed into Lloyd Triestino when the Austrians left, are now government offices: wistfully the marble tritons blow their horns, regretfully Neptune and Mercury linger upon their entablatures. Those silken and epauletted passengers, with all they represented, have vanished from the face of Europe, and I am left all alone listening to the band.

FIVE

Origins of a Civic Style

In the 1970s I once called upon Baron Rafaelle Douglas de Banfield-Tripcovich in his office at the Teatro Verdi. He was the musical director there, besides being a well-known composer. He struck me as an elegant, worldly, very gentlemanly man, dealing with his affairs in an eminently civilized way—a call from a colleague of the international opera circuit ("Of course, Maestro, see you in Paris")—an inquiry from his secretary ("Be so good as to tell them that I may be a few moments late")—matters of score, repertoire or musicianship—a brief exchange about party attitudes in the City Council, where he sat as an independent member. Half-way through my visit he took me over to the window surveying the bay below, and pointed out a stocky little vessel chugging across the harbour towards the mooring berths. "There goes one of my boats," he said, for as it happened he owned all the Trieste tugs, too.

His was the heritage of an earlier Trieste, a style. Behind the pompous and entertaining façade of the imperial seaport, the waltzes, the uniforms, the Revoltellas and the royal visits, there had arisen over the generations a cultivated bourgeoisie. This was the class of society which had, in my view, held the balance of civilization everywhere, tempering the arrogance of aristocracy, restraining the crudity of the masses. In Trieste it made of a working seaport one of Europe's more lively and enlightened cities. Here it was an alliance between business and intellect, perhaps a conscious effort to raise the sights of this money-town towards higher things than profit—the Trieste poet Scipio Slataper, who was killed in the first world war, pictured his city waking up one day "between a crate of lemons and a sack of coffee beans" and suddenly realizing its lack of culture. Doubtless the same misgivings had been felt in Chicago, say, where the wealth and confidence made in steel, slaughter-houses and railroads, and the meeting of clever people from many countries, created museums and art galleries, a great university and a celebrated orchestra: or in Manchester, a hard-headed cotton capital, also full of foreigners, that supported the Hallé Orchestra and the *Manchester Guardian*. The governing class of Trieste in its heyday was rich and complex, and its tradition of involvement in civic affairs survives to this day.

This gives one the feeling that local people, rooted in Trieste, still run the city, in a composed way they no longer do in most cities of the western world. It is not strictly true—in Trieste today outside interests, often foreign, control many an old institution—but there are still prominent citizens whose lives overlap the several spheres, economic and artistic, social and political. It is a tradition here. In the 1760s the Count von Königsbrunn was not only Trieste's chief of police, but also its theatre director: in the 1830s Josef Ressel was not only a forester, botanist and conservationist, but also the inventor of screw propulsion for ships; in our own time there has been

Baron Banfield-Tripcovich and also Ricardo Illy, Mayor of the city at the start of the twenty-first century. Illy is a lightly-built man of contemporary elegance, a style-setter who never wears a tie with his beautifully modish suits, even to the most formal of functions. He is also a highly imaginative politician. And if he looks out of *his* window, as the Maestro-Baron did that day, he is almost sure to see, or at least smell, signs of his own supporting fortune: Illy is one of the great coffee names of the world, and the Mayor's family company is a mainstay of the Trieste economy.

A COLOURFUL and polyglot proletariat sustained Trieste in its boom days. Every travelling writer mentions its vivacity. The port was by far its chief employer, and men and women from many parts worked in the docks—Albanians, Turks, earringed fisher-people from the Venetian lagoons, giant Montenegrins, Greeks with baggy trousers and Byronic headgear—talking and squabbling and singing in many languages, drinking in their particular taverns, living in their specific quarters of town. They ran the stalls of the city markets. They crowded the sidewalks for religious processions. They jammed the variety shows that were performed in pubs and cafés all over town, and they were exuberant celebrants of Carnival. In their varied peasant costumes, their headscarfs and gaudy waistcoats, they gave the place a constant splash of colour.

There was also a remnant of that ancient aristocracy, the Thirteen Families, the Four Hundred of Trieste. They were called Argento, Baseggio, Bellim, Bonomo, Burlo, Cogitti, Giuliani, Leo, Padovine, Pelligrini, Petazzi, Stella and Toffani. Some still lived at their ancestral addresses in the Old City, where the grandest of them still maintained private chapels, but none of their thirteen sonorous names figure prominently in the annals of Habsburgian Trieste. The last descendant of the Giuliani family, in his youth a philosopher and scientist of repute, died in the city in 1835 all alone and forgotten, and in my imagination I see his peers flitting pale and emaciated through their shadowy lanes while the city erupts into fame around them.

Both classes are unrecognizable now, the vibrant multilingual work force, the attenuated medieval aristocracy. Behind and above them both, though, was that well-heeled business society, solid and earnest, and it flourishes still. It was drawn from many of the peoples that had created the new Trieste, and was sprinkled with nobility old and new. Like the governing classes of Chicago and Manchester, it interested itself assiduously in the arts. The city was rich in theatres and concert-halls, and nothing was too high-brow for their audiences. Ibsen, Strindberg, Wagner were all much admired in Trieste. Toscanini, Nikisch and Mahler all conducted here. One of the very first subscribers to Joyce's bewilderingly demanding *Ulysses* was the Triestine Greek entrepreneur Ambrogio Ralli, who had to read the book in English, and without any of the explanatory glosses that have alone made it intelligible to most of us. The City Library, with a famous collection of books and manuscripts, was always busy; the Conservatoire of Music was never short of pupils; language schools were in great demand—even Esperanto was popular; the Università Popolare, although it was not really a university, offered public lectures that were attended by thousands of citizens. Scores of cultural institutions flourished, from the scholarly society called the Gabinetto Minerva to debating clubs and a civic madrigal society. Lloyd Adriatico took time off from the ocean trade to publish a series of classic literature. When the Trieste Yacht Works found that a debtor could not pay the bill for his boat repairs, its directors accepted an Egyptian sarcophagus instead, and passed it on to the city.

Opera was immensely popular, and the masterly beadle at the Teatro Verdi, calling up carriages in his powdered wig, was one of the city's archetypal characters. The opera house itself was a distinguished institution, with a roster of eminent conductors. It was the first anywhere to rename itself after Verdi, and two of his works had their first performances in it (patrons preferred to forget that he didn't bother to attend the opening night of one, *Il Corsaro,* and later rewrote the other, *Stiffelio* ...). The business families of Trieste were fervent opera-goers. When Joyce went to a performance, to sit among the "sour reek of armpits" and "phosphorescent farts" of the upper balcony, he often saw in the stalls and boxes below bourgeois pupils of his, following the music with extreme attention: they had probably read the libretto beforehand, and very likely knew the scores too.

These were the great days of the Viennese cafés, as ubiquitous and as popular here as they were in the capital. Trieste was always a bar town, a restaurant town (though hardly a gourmet's paradise) and especially a coffee-shop town. There had been at least one hundred licensed cafés as early as 1830, and some of them still survive—the Historic Cafés of Trieste, as the tourist people call them now. The Tommaseo, the degli Specchi, the Tergeste, the Stella Polare, the San Marco, all date from Habsburg times, and maintain the high bourgeois tradition. The most suggestive of them is the Caffè San Marco, which is where students and writers still like to drink, talk, work and show themselves off to visitors. When I enter its doors out of the noisy Via Battisti, I feel I am among just the same customers, *mutatis mutandis,* as would have been there a century ago: the students with their text-books spread around them, the professors reading the day's newspapers, the odd author sucking his pen meditatively over his novel, a scattering of ladies enjoying their daily coffee-talk and one or two flaky philosophers with spectacles, sitting there hour after hour gazing at Time. If the empire still existed, an habitué once remarked to the writer Claudio Magris (as recorded in his book *Microcosms*), "the world would still be a Caffè San Marco, and don't you think that's something, if you take a look out there?"

It was a fine time and place for promenading, too. Trieste women were famously well-dressed, in local variants of Vienna fashions, and were good at showing themselves off. They loved to walk their husbands along the sea on summer evenings, or catch the tram up to the Obelisk to saunter along the ridge, or take an educational stroll around the city's fountains, or (a favourite evening recreation) visit the extraordinary collection of oriental *objets d'art* that Adolf Wünsch from Moravia displayed above his pasticceria on the Corso. Families would spend a day picnicking in the hill-side park that Baron Revoltella had bequeathed to the city, where the grown-ups could pay their respects to the magnate and his mother, safe in their tombs in their private chapel, while the children could play for hours with the turtles in the pool outside.

. . .

THE LEGACIES of this society are still inescapable in Trieste. The families may be extinct, but many of their names are still part of the civic vocabulary, and sometimes their memories live. "Who's that?" I asked the man behind the counter at the Cosulich Travel Agency on the Via Rossini, pointing to a photograph of a prosperous-looking gentleman on the wall behind his back. "That's one of the bosses," he said—and he was referring to the Cosulich brothers, shipowners who died generations before he was born.

One can still follow the trails of those happy promenades. Revoltella's chapel reminds me of one of those memorial churches that Russians used to erect on battlefields in the days of the Czars, and the turtles are still a delight. The Opicina tram still braves the 26 percent gradient up to the Obelisk, shoved along in the steepest part by a funicular engine. Even a tour of the city fountains can still be fun. Like most such nineteenth-century merchant cities Trieste was lavishly ornamented with civic fountains, but their careers have been precarious because they have constantly been moved as times or tastes have demanded. One year they are spouting in the Piazza della Borsa, the next they are in the Piazza Venezia—I once chanced to see a mobile crane in the very act of lifting the mountainous centre-piece of the Fountain of the Four Continents, to shift it from one spot to another in the Piazza Unità. The one symbolical fountain-figure that can feel reasonably safe is the little putto in the Piazza Ponterosso, beside the Canal Grande: but then Giovannini del Ponterosso has been there since 1753, before bourgeois Trieste existed, and he has long been so beloved among Triestini of all classes that his tenure seems secure.

Most of the civic statuary proudly commemorates the old bourgeoisie, and properly represents its values. My own tastes run to swagger in public monuments—a few admirals and equestrian generals, a duke or two, soldiers indomitable in life, magnificent in death. Habsburg Trieste was not a swaggering city, though, and its Valhalla is reserved for worthies, preferably respectable and responsible citizens of art or learning. Its earthly annexe is the Public Garden at the top of the Via Cesare Battisti, whose gates are guarded by the grandest worthy of them all. Domenico Rossetti, who died in 1842, was of aristocratic origin actually, but as journalist, scholar, historian, humanist, antiquarian and public benefactor he became the great champion of the bourgeois civilization in Trieste. He gave valuable books to the City Library, he founded the Gabinetto Minerva, he financed the tree-shaded boulevard now called Viale XX Settembre, which is still a pleasant place to sit on a hot day and write a philological thesis. Near the top of it is the Politeama Rossetti, one of the city's two main theatres, and Rossetti himself stands in bronze sentinel over the main gate of the nearby garden. There he is, complacent on his pedestal with a cloak romantically over his shoulders and a forefinger keeping his place in a book, while clambering about his plinth, and flying over it, nymphs or graces reach out to him with olive branches and a flaming torch.

Sheltering behind this high priest of the culture are less executive acolytes. There are twenty-one of them, writers, artists, educators, scientists, musicians, each with his own portrait bust beneath the trees. Most of them are known only in Trieste, a few are internationally famous, but they all stand there, spattered by pigeons, attended by many cats, serenaded by ducks from the duck-pond, with an air of grave dependability. Even Joyce, the one outsider among them, is somehow admitted to the Establishment by the provision of a bronze picture-frame around his head.

ALL IN all Habsburg Trieste was a complete and interesting city, and its citizens were proud of it. Theirs was an age of burgeoning, confident municipalities throughout the industrialized world, with strong municipal governments that made some of them almost city-states. In Trieste the degree of autonomy achieved long before was transmuted into something called *municipalismo,* a conscious sense of separateness that still exists. This was an innovative, technological place, not hampered by nostalgia, and like the Chicagos and the Manchesters it looked eagerly to the future. Its young intellectuals were much taken with the ideas of the Futurist Filippo Marinetti, who believed in a fresh start for everything, artistically, politically, socially, historically. Marinetti in return thought of Trieste as an ideal model for his explosive theories, and called it *la nostra bella polveriera,* "our beautiful powder-magazine." In 1910 a great Futurist meeting was held in the Politeama Rossetti, and half the local intelligentsia attended it. Most of them thought Marinetti went rather too far in demanding the burning of libraries and the flooding of museums, but nevertheless he was right in judging this a society by no means shackled in tradition.

Trieste had its own language, and this helped to heighten the sense of civic completeness. *Triestino* was descended from the Venetian dialect, and was similarly rich in slur and sibilant, but it had absorbed words and idioms from the many other languages of this municipal melting-pot (*sonababic* meant "son-of-a-bitch"). It was not simply a lingua franca of the uneducated, but was commonly used by people of all ranks and resources, in many subtle inflexions—even the Austrians had their own version of it, known as *Austriacans.* Poetry was written in it, speeches were made in it, and to understand it was a mark of civic membership (James Joyce was fluent, and apparently made use of it in the neo-language of *Finnegans Wake*).

The dialect lives on, and so does the familial kind of civic identity. Educated, respectable middle-class citizens still set the style of Trieste, and mould much of its life in their own image. Remember those comfortable rentiers and professionals we saw at their victuals on our first evening in Trieste? I may have been wrong about them, for when I dined there on another evening a table-full of citizens just as respectable, just as discreet, turned out to be writers one and all. Conversely I may be wrong about the customers at the Caffè San Marco too—those professors are probably company accountants really, the novelist is preparing a computer programme and the sages are not contemplating Time, but waiting for the football on TV. With this superficial homogenization goes a more real general pride in the city, and interest in it. Hundreds turn out when they are asked to help clean up the city streets. Books and pamphlets about Trieste pour from the local presses: one published in 1999 contained a local general knowledge quiz, asking for instance who was represented in the marble sculpture in the atrium of the Revoltella Museum (the nymph Aurisina), and how many ice-cream parlours there were in the Viale XX Settembre (five).

By contemporary European standards this is still a calm and self-controlled city. It is one of the few big commercial centres of the continent that was not half-destroyed during the second world war, and in many ways its nineteenth-century moderation has survived. I happened to be sitting on a bench one day when a Chinese man had a heart attack on the seat next door. His wife was distraught, but the responses of passers-by were steady. One man gently laid the poor fellow out on the bench, and propped up his head with a rucksack. Another comforted the weeping wife. A third ran off to call the emergency services, and in a matter of moments, with a minimum of fuss, a woman doctor and two stalwart para-medics arrived to whisk the man away to hospital. "Who must I pay?" asked the wife helplessly. "Nobody, Madame," she was proudly told, "it is a service of our city."

Can it all last? Young people tell me they find the civic ethos oppressive. Others say it is being whittled away by the influx of migrants from Italy, who bring with them what one informant defined for me as *caosmismo,* chaoticness. Certainly the Trieste bourgeoisie seems to get older every year. Watch its representatives, any fine summer day, going down for their morning dalliances at the outdoor cafés beside the Canal Grande, with their sticks and spectacles and sunhats and little dogs on leads, and you may well think them a dying caste. I once came across a open-air concert in the Piazza della Borsa where a few hundred of them had assembled. From the waterfront there sounded, on the evening air, the thump of a rap band, but in the piazza all was fond sentimentality. The performer was a well-known Trieste artist called Umberto Lupi, who sang songs in the Trieste dialect. He was of a certain age himself, and he sat at his keyboard altogether relaxed, in shirt and slacks and anorak, while before him his elderly audience responded as they might to a family friend. They knew him well, and he knew them. As he sang they sang with him, laughed with him, swayed and tapped their feet as he did.

They were singing their own songs, in their own language, out of their own past. I noticed that some of their eyes were full of tears, and I almost wept a little myself: because of their age, because of mine, because of the hard times they had lived through, because Signor Lupi was a true professional, because of the sweet songs, because I feared that nobody would be singing them much longer, because of the decline of the bourgeosie across the world, and because—well, because of the Trieste effect.

TO CELEBRATE the start of the third millennium the whole of the Piazza Unità, the largest square in Italy, was officially painted over with an enormous picture to mark Trieste's place in Europe. It showed a brave young woman, blond hair flying, riding a bull towards the open sea, with a sun and a moon above, and seven stars against an azure sky. Hundreds of citizens, young and old, had helped to spread its four tons of blue, yellow, red and white paint over the surface of the square, and they had been encouraged to add a thousand slogans and messages of their own, so that the whole was like the biggest graffito ever scrawled. Nobody could see all of it, except from a helicopter, and people wandered the piazza all day long, exploring the different corners of this communal signature.

The Irish-Triestine scholar John McCourt (to whose book

The Years of Bloom I am much indebted) has likened the Trieste dialect to "a living encyclopedia of the cultures, nations and languages that had been assimilated by the city." In the same way I thought the millennium painting in the Piazza Unità a proper index of the city's character (and I considered it only proper, too, in a city of intelligent dialectic, that the management of the Caffè degli Specchi, which was obliged to close its doors during the months it took to clean everything off and resurface the square, should have declared the whole project just another example of The Arrogance of Power).

SIX

Sad Questions of Oneself

On July 2, 1914, the 22,000-ton battleship SMS *Viribus Unitis* arrived at the Molo San Carlo in Trieste bringing the corpses of the Archduke Franz Ferdinand, nephew and heir to the Emperor, and his wife, Sophie. They had both been assassinated at Sarajevo, in the Austrian territory of Bosnia-Herzegovina, five days before.

Their coffins were carried in funeral procession through the streets of Trieste, before being sent by train to Vienna. This was an imperial frisson of an altogether new kind, and I can sense the shock of the occasion from an old photograph I have before me now. Sailors line the street, imperial infantrymen escort the cortège, led by mounted officers with cockaded hats. Every window and balcony, attic to ground floor, is crowded with people. Black flags or carpets hang from walls and flagstaffs. A mass of citizenry fills the pavements, the women in dark clothes, the men removing from their heads the boaters which every self-respecting male wore in summer Trieste. The photograph was taken by the local photographers Giuseppe and Carlo Wulz, whose very names give it a true Trieste evocation.

At the moment they clicked their shutter the procession has

momentarily halted in the Corso, the main street of the city, now the Corso Italia. There is no apparent reason. Everybody in the crowd, from every window, is looking towards the coffins. The soldiers are rigid. The officers have turned in their saddles to see what is happening. Beside the bier a solitary courtier stands motionless, his top hat in his hand. Soldiers, sailors, citizens, officials, all wait still, silent and expectant. Did some of them guess that the saddest of angel messengers was passing by, foretelling the world's tragedy, the empire's humiliation, and their own proud city's long decline?

IT WAS when those bodies returned from Sarajevo, I suppose, that tristesse was decreed for Trieste, but long before then melancholy had found its proper image here. Miramar contains its very essence. It stands on its promontory weeping, and to my eyes even in the sunshine its walls are never sparkling. A pleasant park surrounds it, and its rooms are full of treasures, but nobody who goes there can fail to sense its numen of regret.

Maximilian, having ably reformed the Austrian Navy, retired from the sea in 1856, but he did not get on well with his elder brother the Emperor, and was happy to live well away from Vienna with his devoted young bride. He was a dreamy sort of man, somewhat liberal in his views and much influenced by his uncle the crazed romantic Ludwig I of Bavaria, so he was not at ease with the stiff autocracy of *K u K*. He was actually removed from a post as Governor-General of Lombardy as being too progressive (and a good thing too, perhaps, for he wanted to plant the Piazza San Marco at Venice with orange trees, and turn its campanile into a lighthouse).

However, in 1864 he was called to take part in a fateful imperialist scheme. The French had suggested to Franz Joseph that to counter the growing strength of the United States, there should be an attempt to re-establish European sovereignty on the American continent. The idea was that with French military support a European monarchy should be restored to the throne of a key Latin American republic, Mexico. This was in the hands of a left-wing revolutionary, Benito Juárez, and there was thought to be a strong conservative faction in the country in favour of such an intervention. Besides, it was the nearest of all the republics to Washington. The Americans were in the throes of their civil war, and probably distracted from the principles of the Monroe Doctrine: an alliance might perhaps be struck with the Confederate States of the South, much more sympathetic to European ways and monarchical instincts than were Abraham Lincoln's modernist northerners.

A French expedition accordingly invaded Mexico, drove Juárez out of Mexico City, installed a puppet administration and awaited a new Emperor of Mexico from Europe. Who better to send than Maximilian the Habsburg, with Carlotta of the Belgians as his Empress? His love-castle at Trieste was not yet completed, the trees were still saplings that he had planted with his own hand, the last of the ornamental statuary had yet to be installed in the park, when a Mexican deputation arrived at Miramar to offer him the throne. Maximilian was understandably reluctant, but he obeyed his brother's wishes and sailed off with Carlotta to Mexico in the 2,600-ton frigate *Novara,* recently converted from sail to steam in a Trieste shipyard. He was never to see his Miramar again, for the French presently deserted him, the Mexicans put him against a wall and shot him, and Carlotta was left to return to Europe and go mad.

The castle, its name now Italianized as Miramare, is Maximilian's only remaining memorial in Trieste: that statue of him outside Revoltella's house was eventually pulled down after all, and stands today in the castle park. Miramare is a museum now, and full of grief. Its lavish royal trophies are pathetically ironic—none more so than the crimson canopied bed that Napoleon III gave Maximilian and Carlotta as a wedding present, or the marble-topped table, a present from Pope Pius X, upon which Maximilian had signed his suicidal commitment to the Mexicans. Two big celebratory pictures by dell'Acqua hang in the castle's Historical Room, to pile on the agony. In one Maximilian, in a brass-buttoned frock coat, is accepting from a respectful huddle of Mexican functionaries, including the Archbishop of Mexico City, the invitation to become their Emperor. In another the Archdukely couple , standing in a barge rowed by bearded sailors and flying an imperial ensign, are offering a restrained goodbye to a crowd of well-wishers on the castle steps, while a second, less dignified audience waves its hats from the jetty beyond. Boat-crews salute with raised oars, and off-shore the frigate awaits them dressed overall.

The castle has often been unlucky, and gloomy legend attends it. The Empress Elizabeth, Franz Joseph's consort, often stayed there, and was eventually stabbed to death at Geneva. Carlotta briefly lived there, and in the end went off her head. The German Kaiser Wilhelm II stayed there once, and soon had to abdicate his throne. The first King of Albania spent a few nights there, and his throne lasted only six months. The Duke of Aosta sailed away from Miramare to be Italian Viceroy of Ethiopia, and never returned to Italy. When the British General Bernard Freyberg chose it as his headquarters at the end of the second world war he preferred to be on the safe side, and slept in the garden; but one of his American successors defied superstition and was later killed in Korea, and another died in a car crash on his way back to Trieste from the United States.

For me looking out from Miramare's luxurious drawing-rooms, hung with chandeliers and royal portraits, and equipped with tinted windows to add lustre to the view—looking across the empty water to the city of Trieste is almost an ecstasy of the poignant. Once when I was there a frightful thunder-storm burst, and a few raindrops seeped through the ceiling of the castle's throne room to fall heavily on the floor: only a few of us were present, and with silent respect we stood around the spot as the water slowly and rhythmically fell—drip, drop, drip, drop, like the sad ticking of time. Shortly before he died Maximilian wrote from Mexico ordering two thousand nightingales to be sent to him from Miramar, and I can still imagine them, freed from their cages, fluttering westward out to sea.

ARISTOTLE, I have been told, believed that every interesting man possessed a streak of melancholy. I feel the same about cities, and in this respect Trieste is a winner. Melancholy is Trieste's chief rapture. In almost everything I read about this city, by writers down the centuries, melancholy is evoked. It is not a stabbing sort of disconsolation, the sort that makes you pine for death (although Trieste's suicide rate, as a matter of fact, is notoriously high). In my own experience it is more like our Welsh *hiraeth,* expressing itself in bitter-sweetness and a yearning for we know not what.

Even Marcel Proust, who never visited Trieste, has his Narrator think of it as "a delicious place in which the people were pensive, the sunsets golden, the church bells melancholy." Umberto Saba, the Trieste poet *in excelsis,* seems to have been habitually melancholic in the city he loved: he thought the street called Lazaretto Vecchio "mirrors me in my long days of closed sorrow," on the Molo San Barlo he could "dream my days were almost happy," and when in exile he remembered a time in Trieste when he *was* happy, even then he felt obliged to add "God forgive me that great tremendous word." The German novelist Ricarda Huch said the melancholy of Trieste affected her more than its beauty, so that only when she went home did she remember "the way the crest of the Karst disappeared in a shimmering of violet into the horizon." Even Italo Svevo's great Trieste novel *La Coscienza di Zeno,* which is often very funny, is infused with a haunting sense of unfulfilment.

The very sea of Trieste, although it lies very beautifully beneath the hills, seldom seems to me a laughing sea. Some seas are different in character every day, with the light, the tide and the ripples, but Trieste's sea invariably strikes me as *brooding.* In winter it can suggest somewhere cruel, on the Black Sea, or in the Baltic. On a hot summer day it can acquire an unearthly stillness; the sky merges metallically with the water, ships stand leaden on the horizon and one can't quite make out where the hull of a moored boat ends, and its reflection begins. Nowhere can be much more peaceful than the bay at dead of night, with only a few motionless lights of fishing-boats about, a faint insomniac hum from the city, and a tinny clang when Michez and Jachez wake up to clash the passing of another hour; yet somehow or other, through it all, the sea of Trieste broods away the aeons, rain or shine, light or dark.

Trieste makes one ask sad questions of oneself. What am I here for? Where am I going? It had this effect upon me when I was in my teens; now that I am in my seventies, in my jejune way I feel it still.

HISTORY is one source of these sensations—*men are we, and must grieve when even the shade of that which once was great has passed away.* Isolation is another. Trieste still stands out on a limb, and even in the age of the web and the television, its young people in particular often feel cut off from the life of the great world: at the start of the twenty-first century Munich was the only city outside Italy which had direct scheduled flights to Trieste.

More directly, though, an uneasy climate is probably the cause. Summer is seldom decorative here, but more often hangs heavy and sullen on the city, malignantly bronzing the sun-bathers who lie in their hundreds on the corniche of Barcola, between the city and Miramare. "The damned monotonous summer," Joyce called it, and I remember with horror the mosquitoes which, high on San Giusto's hill, used to hurl themselves at the mosquito nets of my youth. But the winter's the thing. In particular it is given a baleful excitement by the terrific Trieste phenomenon called the bora (a dialect variant of the Latin *boreas,* the north wind). This ferocious wind from the east-north-east long ago became fundamental to Trieste's self-image. There is a street named after it in the Old City. The pine-woods on the slopes of the Karst were planted specifically to shield the city from it. Sometimes railway wagons used to be blown over by it, and long ago in some streets railings were attached to the walls for pedestrians to hang on to. Trieste makes the most of its bora. On the wind-rose at the end of the Molo Audace, on the central waterfront, the four conventional Mediterranean winds occupy their usual places on the roundel, but the bora is all alone, away at the edge, a wind spectacularly on its own. Local historians assure us that the outcome of a battle fought up on the Karst in A.D. 394 was so affected by a bora—they call it the Battle of the Bora—that it led directly to the end of the Roman Empire.

Citizens love their visitors to encounter this most Triestine of experiences, and they have celebrated the bora in wry art and anecdote. The artist Carlo Wostry, who died in 1943 and declared it to be "the only original thing we have," did a famous series of bora cartoons—skirts flying, top hats tumbling, horses halted in their tracks, papers whisked about all over the place and women huddling in phalanx to keep themselves upright. They say the bora is cyclical, and blew less frequently in the last decades of the twentieth century, but when one morning I opened my curtains in the first year of the twenty-first, I was delighted to see the old monster whipping through the trees below, sending the leaves scudding madly across the sidewalks and boiling the lethargic sea.

However, whenever down the years I have been caught by the bora in full blast, it has left me strangely disturbed. I love demonstrations of nature in the raw, but when this fearful zephyr has howled away I feel curiously enervated or desolate. Stendhal, in 1839, defined the sensation as rheumatism in his entrails, and perhaps it is the source of Trieste's endemic hypochondria. Imaginary illnesses have always been prevalent here, in literature as in life. Svevo's fictional *alter ego* Zeno suffers every kind, eventually reaching the conclusion that a *maladie imaginaire* is worse than the real thing because it is incurable. During his stay here James Joyce experienced as many fanciful afflictions as real ones, and I myself, as I write, seem to feel a peculiarly developing pain in my right ear-lobe. I was once woken in the night by a portentous flashing of lights through my window. Rushing to my balcony I saw that offshore a great cruise ship was standing, brilliantly illuminated, while below me on the quay, lights were blinking urgently on a police car and a white ambulance. A passenger on the ship was being brought ashore for surgery; but ominous though the spectacle was, and awful his predicament, as I returned sleepy to my bed I could not help wondering if, being where he was when the emergency seized him, he was not fancying the whole thing.

Imagine the accumulated psychological deposits of a million boras, deposited in this city over the millennia and augmented by sundry more tangible despairs, and it is not surprising that in recent times Trieste has not been naturally blithe.

IT WAS not always so. Before the gods of capitalism adopted Trieste, before it was properly Austrianized, visitors thought it a regular beaker-full of the warm south, joyous with Latin vivacity.

The young German architect Karl Friedrich Schinkel, arriving in 1803 and still half aghast at the awfulness of the Karst, was delighted by its lively night-life. Soon afterwards a Romanian traveller, Dinco Golescu, felt much the same, and wrote of a city brilliant with great lanterns, and an opera audience of three thousand so moved by the performance of the evening, and so emotionally uninhibited, "that I hardly saw one hundred who did not have to wipe their eyes." Nowadays not so many Triestini cry in public, even when Signor Lupi is singing, and going to the opera is not the heart-on-sleeve experience it can be in more Italianate parts of Italy. Over the years I have spent five or six evenings at the Teatro Verdi, just on impulse, and I have found myself content but not exhilarated.

This is partly because twice the opera of the night has happened to be a work by a local composer, Antonio Smareglia (1854–1929), whose operas are hardly ever performed anywhere else. But it is also, to risk a generalization, because of the modern Trieste temperament, bred by history out of race. This is an audience courteous, interested, informed, but hardly demonstrative. Its response is measured. People don't wipe their eyes much in these stalls, no claques break into hysterical applause. Divas need not expect mid-aria encouragement. There is no wild covey of music students in the upper balconies, as ready to boo as to cheer, and when we all file out into the night not a soul is going to be whistling that love-aria from Act 2 (not even me, if only because, not being very familiar with the melodies of Smareglia, I can't remember how it goes).

. . .

NO MORE, never again," is the refrain that haunts the last pages of Svevo's tragic novel *Senilità*. It is a refrain of Trieste itself, embodied in the presence of Miramare, and James Joyce caught its melancholy in a poem. "Watching the Needle-Boats at San Sabba" is about watching the sculling-crews which in his time, as in ours, were often to be seen training or racing in the waters of the two bays:

> I heard their young hearts crying
> Loveward above the glancing oar
> And heard the prairie grasses sighing
> No more, return no more.
>
> O hearts, O sighing grasses,
> Vainly your loveblown bannerets mourn!
> No more will the wild wind that passes
> Return, no more return.

The water was calm and still that day, I feel sure, and the poet could perhaps hear the hard breathing of the oarsmen above the swish of their oars. He could also hear in his head the last chorus of Puccini's *La Fanciulla del West*, "The Girl of the Golden West," so full of plangent yearning. *Mai più ritornarai, mai più* . . . Half a century later I heard that same refrain on a trading schooner anchored in the bay of Trieste, within sight of Maximilian's castle. Two of us had gone on board to visit its captain, taking with us a couple of bottles of sparkling *prosecco* wine. We sat there drinking while the sun went down, and as the dusk fell upon Miramare the captain softly sang to himself that very phrase—*"Mai più ritornarai, mai più"*: "No more, return no more!"

SEVEN

Trains on the Quays

Until the 1950s freight trains ran along Trieste's central waterfront, connecting the Sudbahn station at the northern end with the Campo Marzio station at the southern—each the terminus of a separate system. The tracks are still there, with a turntable halfway along, but the southern station is now a railway museum, and nowadays trains going to the industrial quarter and the modern docks on Muggia bay pass through an inland tunnel. I miss the trains on the quays. With their panting steam locomotives and their clanking wagons they passed slowly along the waterfront, and often workmen sat on their flat-topped wagons, hitching a ride from one siding to another. They were shabby, noisy old trains. When Gustav Mahler, staying at the Hôtel de la Ville, complained about the mercantile racket of the city, it was probably because he was kept awake by their pantings, whistlings and rusty squeaks outside his window.

Sometimes, even on spring days, there used to be a crust of snow on those passing trucks, and this seemed pathetically metaphorical to me. Snow from where, I used to wonder? Snow from Carpathia, from Bohemia, from the Vienna woods?

By the time it reached Trieste it was broken and grubby at the edges, mouldering at the heart, and struck me as sad stuff. It was like snow sent into exile, banished from its bright cold uplands, wherever they were, to drip into oblivion in this grey enclave by the sea.

The trains themselves made me think of exile, too, for there is nothing more evocative of goodbyes than the sound, look and smell of trains. When you see people off at an airport you know they can be home again in a few hours, but a last kiss at an international railway station is like a premonition of infinity. My own archetypal exile is the Russian writer Ivan Bunin, author of *The Gentleman from San Francisco,* who lived outside his own country for the last forty years of his life, and who, if he was never in Trieste, certainly ought to have been. Bunin was haunted by trains until the end of his days, seeing in them reminders, I suppose, of his homeland's immense track-crossed spaces, the heart-rending gaps of time between departures and arrivals, partings and reunions.

He would have been among friends in Trieste, for this is a city made for exiles. Many exiles, of course, are given no choice, but I imagine most of us sometimes tire of living in the open, where everything is plain to see and we ourselves are obvious, and for anyone with this sporadic impulse to withdraw into somewhere less transparent, Trieste offers a compelling destination—surreptitious itself, and ambiguous. It has offered a new home to many expatriates, voluntary or compulsory, but in the event many have spent half their time here wistfully wishing they were somewhere else. For this is an ironic gift of the place—to attract and to sadden, both at the same time. You can hardly come to Trieste without responding to its natural beauties—the sea at its best so profoundly blue, Miramare wistful on its promontory, Istria running away like a mirage to the south and the harsh hills of the Karst a tantalizing backdrop. But then that train goes by, with that layer of old snow, to remind you that you are far away.

FAR AWAY from where? Exile is no more than absence, and it can take many forms. Some say a sense of exile is built into us when we are weaned from our mothers' breasts; others that it begins when we are told for the first time to leave the family table, or are left self-conscious and apprehensive at our first children's party. At the other end of life I have often met exiles from their own times. I think of old British colonialists, bred to authority and the wide horizons, living out their pensioned lives in semi-detached houses of cramped suburbia. I met a man in Mississippi who subsisted, all too late, in one of those great ante-bellum mansions of the Old South, looked after by a single black woman instead of a dozen house-slaves, still talking about steamboats, balls and thoroughbred horses, and eating his fried chicken off a bedsheet. In Stalin's Leningrad I found myself minded, courtesy of the KGB, by a woman of such exquisite aristocratic grace that she seemed to have stepped straight out of a ball-room of Czarist St. Petersburg. In India I met an old English couple who were so wedded to the lost Raj that they were spending their last years in the stables of a Punjabi racecourse, drinking tea out of chipped mugs and recalling glittering meets of long before.

For myself, absence from place is the truest exile. I first experienced its pangs when I was sent away to boarding-school—exile was mine when, rising that first morning from prickly institutional blankets in a loveless dormitory, I crept to the window and saw outside a totally unknown landscape. Bunin in his exile pined not so much for Russian life as for Russia itself, because being far from the place you love can mean more than being far from the people you love. "Oh what have I done," a nineteenth-century English imperialist was heard groaning from his bed, during a tour of duty in the generally delightful Ionian island of Cephalonia, "oh *what* have I done, that Her Majesty should banish me to this vile and abominable place?" Countless other expatriates, of all nationalities and in all ages, have cried the same, when the incurable and sometimes unaccountable longing for a homeland seizes them, and many of them have groaned it in Trieste.

NAMELESS foreigners by the thousand have come to Trieste and lived here happily ever after—all those Greeks, Armenians and Turks of the Habsburg port, some of them so delighted to be here that before they had houses, they lived on boats in the harbour. Many of Trieste's more famous expatriates, though, have not been content for very long. Waring himself, their poetic prototype, did not linger—his original was a poet named Alfred Domett who ended up as Prime Minister of New Zealand. Richard Coeur de Lion probably never came at all: legend says he was imprisoned here on his way from the Holy Land, and Arco Ricardo, the Roman arch we passed on the way up San Giusto hill, is supposed to have been called after him, but scholars scoff. Casanova stuck it here for two years between 1772 and 1774, having by his own account a pleasant enough stay, but as soon as the Procurators of Venice allowed him to go home, he was off within the week.

The Austrian artist Egon Schiele came for a time, recovering from the effects of a short jail sentence, but he painted only a few watercolours of the harbour before hastening back to Vienna. And the German art historian and archaeologist Johann Winckelmann, "the Father of Neo-Classicism," stayed in this city only eight days, because having arrived on June 1, 1768, he was murdered on June 8, and thus provided the most dramatic of Trieste's exile stories.

Nobody really knows why this world-famous and universally admired scholar was killed. He had made an unhappily abortive visit to Germany from Rome, where he was living. On the way back he had stopped in Vienna, where Maria Theresa presented him with two gold medals, and he had arrived in Trieste planning to take ship to Ancona. He put up at the new Locanda Grande, one of the buildings which then blocked the seaward end of the Piazza Grande. There he apparently made friends with Francesco Arcangeli, a young man staying in the next room, and they spent much of the week strolling the city together. On the eighth day Arcangeli murdered him.

The villain was caught, confessed, turned out to be a convicted thief and was broken on the wheel outside the doors of the hotel, providing it with the ultimate in publicity. His motives remain murky. Perhaps he had planned to steal the gold medals, perhaps he had some obscure political purpose, or perhaps he had embroiled the scholar in a homosexual entanglement. Winckelmann was famously ecstatic about Greek male statuary, "clothed with eternal springtime" and "perfumed by the essence of the gods." Missing his home comforts even at the Grande, perhaps he had found himself a rough companion, had squabbled with him in a moment of jealousy or condescension, and had paid the price twice over.

Nothing could be much sadder—far from his books poor Winckelmann died, far from his pleasant quarters at the Vatican, alone with a young scoundrel on a foreign shore. Classicist that he was, he thought Ulysses a symbol of longing for a fatherland, and in his last moments he must have been horribly homesick too. At the time all educated Europe, we are told, was saddened by the news of his death—"universal mourning and lamentation," Goethe wrote—and the Winckelmann story long ago entered the somewhat meagre tourist repertoire of Trieste. It was Domenico Rossetti who thought of establishing a Lapidary Garden in his memory. It is close to the cathedral, a mellow clutter of slabs and ancient stones in an expanse of rough grass. In one corner stands a cenotaph in Winckelmann's honour, erected under the patronage of an emperor, three kings and a grand duke, containing a fine marble image of Dr. Winckelmann and sundry examples of the busts, torsos, thoughtful muses and fragrant heroes of his enthusiasms.

By now his name is unknown to all but the most erudite visitors, but every tourist is directed to his monument. The great scholar is depicted in a toga, leading towards two ancient sculpted heads the adoring female figures of Architecture, Criticism, History, Philosophy and Sculpture, who are prettily holding hands. Such is Trieste's remorseful tribute to—who was it again? Winkler? Vogelmann? That guy who got murdered? Winckelmann, that's it, Winckelmann, whoever he was.

. . .

EXILED royalty have sometimes found more comfortable refuge in this outpost of an imperial monarchy. It was a convenient substitute for a capital of their own. They would not be patronized, they could be reasonably anonymous if they wished it, there were agreeable villas to buy or rent and Trieste's efficient communications could keep them in touch with affairs and well-wishers at home in Ruritania. Whether of ancient or of upstart blood, they could be fairly sure of respectful treatment, especially if they were rich (which, in the way of dispossessed royalty, they nearly always were).

When two elderly daughters of Louis XV of France, Marie-Adélaïde and Victoire-Louise, arrived in 1797, escaping the revolution, they were accompanied by a large entourage, they were put ashore with a salute of twenty-one guns, they were honoured as Les Mesdames de France, and when they died they were buried ceremonially in the cathedral. Carlists from Spain were equally honoured. In a dim side-chapel of the cathedral a covey of them lies. When they failed to retain the throne of Spain against their Bourbon rivals they had gravitated naturally enough to Urbs Fidelissima, where they could be sure of official hospitality and protection against assassins. How grandly they must have moved through town, when State or Society called them, and how loftily patrician they must have seemed, descended from a hundred crowns, in this city of merchants! The most rigid Spanish etiquette protected them from the vulgar, and they received visitors in audience in a throne room in the Via Lazaretto Vecchio.

In 1922 Ivan Bunin, then living in a dingy villa above Grasse, went down the hill to Antibes to see the lying-in-state of the Grand Duke Nikolai Nikolaevich, brother to the late Czar. He found that Russia itself was reconstituted around the catafalque: incense burnt, choirs chanted, officers of the lost imperial armies were magnificently uniformed, and for an hour or two Bunin felt that he was not in exile at all. In their deaths the Carlists of Trieste fostered the same illusion. They were given solemn stately funerals at San Giusto, with muffled drums and furled flags of Spain: the tomb of the first of them, in their shadowy chapel up there, describes him grandiloquently still as "Carolus V Hispaniorum Rex," and since 1901 the last of them, the pretender Carlos VII, has mouldered in his grave dressed in the full regalia of a Spanish captain-general.

SEVERAL Napoleonic notables spent exiled time in Trieste. Napoleon himself came in 1797, during one of his occupations of the city, but he stayed only a single night. His various myrmidons stayed longer. No doubt they had heard good things of the place from Comte Henri Bertrand, the most faithful Bonapartiste of them all, because he had been briefly Governor of Trieste in his hero's phantasmagorical Province of Illyria, before following him to a less agreeable place of exile. Napoleon's sister Elisa lived here during her brother's last years, and his sister Caroline came here, bringing a niece of his Empress Josephine as governess for her children, and one of the best-known of all the city's refugees was Prince Jérôme, Napoleon's youngest and raciest brother. He was the so-called King of Westphalia, and turned up here in 1814, with a suite of fifty-four courtiers, when Napoleon abdicated in Paris. He was very much a man of the world, and had lived for a time in New York, where he found himself a wife. Napoleon had made him first a general, then a king, annulled his American marriage and wedded him off to a daughter of the King of Württemberg. In Trieste, his own trumped-up monarchy having collapsed, he called himself at first the Comte de Hartz; but when Napoleon escaped from Elba and he himself he went off to share the defeat at Waterloo, he returned to the city as the Prince de Montfort.

Trieste suited Jérôme. He lived splendidly in a villa, not far from the waterfront, that had belonged to "Pharaoh" Cassis but which everyone called the Villa Napoleone; nowadays it is the Villa Necker, the Italian Army's headquarters in the city, with an officers' club attached, and a lush park behind. Jérôme thrived there, fathering three children and buying several ample properties as speculative ventures, and after his years in the city he never looked back. He went home to Paris, where his nephew had become Napoleon III, to be a Marshal of France, Governor of the Invalides and eventually President of the Senate. His son Jérôme Junior, better known to the world as Plon-Plon, was born in Trieste, and a plaque on the side of the Villa Necker acknowledges his loyalty to the city—"Never forget my birthplace Trieste," he is said to have urged King Umberto of Italy, who happened to be his son-in-law. And nearly a century later the quasi-King of Westphalia's grandson Charles, by his unfortunate American wife, became Attorney General of the United States.

SOME celebrated foreigners have come to Trieste to work, and their responses have usually been ambivalent. The French consul Marie-Henri Beyle, for example, posted here in 1830, was decidedly not happy, and it is not surprising. He was forty-seven years old when he was appointed, and since he was well-known for his advanced and outspoken political liberalism, he was hardly likely to be welcomed to their imperial port by the authorities of a reactionary monarchy. Still, he found himself a pleasant house on the city outskirts and he enjoyed the exotic nature of the place, its fine boulevards along the sea, its grand houses, the colourful Slavs and Levantines who frequented its waterfront—"amiable half-savages," he called them, whose talk was "continual poetry." But Trieste soon soured on him. The food was dreadful, the peasants were money-grubbing, the bora debilitated him. The Austrians gave him no peace, censoring his letters and watching all his movements, and after only five months they expelled him. It was his only experience of Trieste, but since he was also known as Stendhal, and within the year had published *Le Rouge et le Noir,* none of it really mattered anyway.

Charles Lever, the Anglo-Irish novelist, was British Consul in Trieste during the 1860s, and his experience of the place was not much happier. When Lord Derby the Foreign Secretary offered him the post it sounded fine—"six hundred a year for doing nothing, and you are just the man to do it." It sounded like a rest cure for a wandering littérateur who normally had to live by his pen, but he soon found Trieste detestable. "Of all the dreary places it has been my lot to sojourn in, this is the worst." The British residents bored him. The only Triestines he knew were dull business people. His heart gave him trouble, the bora blew, his wife died and he was plunged into periods of melancholy. Before he himself died on the job in 1872, he did have time to set a novel in the Trieste region, but it was no *Le*

Rouge et le Noir, and only a few years later his grave in the Protestant cemetery was described as "a rubbish corner of stray papers and old tin pots."

Sigmund Freud was also frustrated here. In a city that later embraced his ideas with particular zeal, being organically inclined towards neurosis, he himself found only failure. He came to Trieste on the train from Vienna in 1876, commissioned by the Institute of Comparative Anatomy at Vienna University to solve a classically esoteric zoological puzzle: how eels copulated. Specialist as he later became in the human testicle and its influence upon the psyche, Freud diligently set out to discover the elusive reproductive organs of *Anguilla anguilla,* whose location had baffled investigators since the time of Aristotle. He did not solve the mystery, but I like to imagine him dissecting his four hundred eels in the institute's zoological station here. Solemn, earnest and bearded I fancy him, rubber-gloved and canvas-aproned, slitting them open one after the other in their slimy multitudes. Night after night I see him peeling off his gloves with a sigh to return to his lonely lodgings, and saying a weary goodnight to the lab assistant left to clear up the mess—"Goodnight, Alfredo," "Goodnight, Herr Doktor. Better luck next time, eh?" But the better luck never came; the young genius returned to Vienna empty-handed, so to speak, but perhaps inspired to think more exactly about the castration complex.

HERE is another cameo of exile's disillusionment. On October 29, 1904, a small lonely figure sat on a bench outside the Sudbahn railway station, at the foot of an obelisk commemorating The Yielding of Trieste to Austria, which showed an allegorical Trieste, head held gratefully high, emerging from a pile of Roman ruins. The obelisk has long gone, but the memorial to the Empress Elizabeth, "Sissy," has lately been re-erected in the garden opposite the station entrance, and it will do just as well for us. There we see the little figure waiting, hour after hour, wearing a bonnet and a well-worn travelling dress, and with bags and bundles on the ground around her. Now and then she glances at the station clock, and she watches anxiously along the road to the city centre. And here at last comes the man she has been waiting for. Tall, skinny, be-spectacled, in a buttoned tweed suit and a straw hat, smelling slightly of liquor, here comes James Joyce to comfort his worried young mistress Nora Barnacle, who jumps to her feet, clutches her hat and runs tearfully to greet him.

She was relieved to see her Jim, of course, but he did not give her an easy time during the years they spent in Trieste. The Joyces came here from Zurich, on the promise of employment at the Berlitz School of Languages, and James left Nora so long beside the railway station that day because almost at once he had got into trouble. He had gone off to find somewhere to stay the night, but instead had promptly fallen in with a drunken party of seamen in the Piazza Grande, and there the police had arrested him. It took a reluctant British Consul to get him out of jail, and poor Nora might well have thought it was a sorry omen for their future in Trieste.

She would have been right. Following them in retrospect through their time in the city is hardly a light-hearted experience. Joyce scratched a living as a teacher of English, partly at the Berlitz, partly privately, but he was hopeless with money, always in debt and frequently in trouble with landlords. Street after street remembers the couple, and you can still follow their progress from one drab apartment to another, first by themselves, then with a baby, then with Joyce's brother Stanislaus, then with a second baby, then with his sister Eva and their two children, then with his sister Eileen—jam-packed, frequently testy and always hard up. They gave up once and went away for a few months to Rome, and they went away again during the first world war, but like so many others, if James Joyce was often disconsolate when he was in Trieste, when he was away from it he often pined for the place.

Nora was the one to be pitied, though, and it is her small waiting figure outside the station that is my own most potent Joycean image of Trieste. Joyce himself had his genius to keep him company. He wrote the whole of *A Portrait of the Artist as a Young Man* in Trieste, and most of *Dubliners,* and he devised much of *Ulysses.* He also made close friends among his pupils and their families, most of them interested in the arts, and became an oddly welcome guest in some of the rich mercantile houses of the city. He even dabbled in business himself—there was a scheme to sell Irish tweed in Trieste, and another to start a chain of cinemas in Ireland. Then his son and daughter gave him great delight, and the city gave him inspiration. He called it Europiccola. He liked wandering its streets. He spent long hours in its churches, especially the Greek Orthodox church of San Nicolo, whose rituals fascinated him. There were hundreds of pubs, cafés and brothels to entertain him, and in general he enjoyed the flavour of *K u K,* which he found "charming and gay."

But Joyce also wrote the play *Exiles* in Trieste. For all his pleasures, it appears, he was never easy in the city, and no doubt this was partly because of Nora. She was bored there—"now I suppose you will think I am very difficult but one cant live only for the sun and the blue Mediteranean sea." She was not in the least interested in Joyce's art, she seldom accompanied him to the houses of his friends or the taverns of his recreation, and year after year she had to keep the household together on skimpy pittances. She was an Irish colleen, born to be merry and reckless, and perhaps in his mind's eye Joyce always saw her, as I do, sitting there beside the monument on that first day, her bags on the ground around her, while the trains whistled sadly behind her back, and he drank with the sailors in the piazza.

During his later time in Trieste Joyce wrote to the young German publisher Kurt Wolff, in Munich, offering to send him an untitled novel he had written. Wolff turned down the unknown author. Long years afterwards he became my own original publisher, but I suspect that if he had published *Ulysses* he would never have bothered with me.

IN SOME ways it seems to me that Joyce and Trieste were made for each other. If Mr. Bloom had not grown up in Dublin he might have been a Triestine. Sandymount Strand might have been the rocks of Barcola, out by Miramare, and Molly might well have opened her legs in some sleazy backstreet of the Old City. Other expatriates in this city, on the contrary, were miserably alien to the temper of the place, and pre-eminent among these was Sir Richard Francis Burton. He was as un-Triestine a character as it is possible to imagine, a spectacularly alarming man who presented himself deliberately to the world as an evil genius, with terrifyingly cold blue eyes to prove it. He had fought and explored all over the world, and besides being a great scholar and the author of celebrated books, he relished every kind of subterfuge and anomaly. He had been to Mecca in disguise; he had explored the homosexual stews of Karachi and investigated the polygamy of the Mormons. He never denied the rumour that in Arabia he had once murdered a man in cold blood.

When in 1872, in his fifty-first year, Her Majesty's Foreign Office chose Burton to represent Queen Victoria in this respectable seaport he was affronted and dismayed. He thought Trieste preposterously unworthy of him. His ideal foreign country was "a haggard land infested with wild beasts and wilder men, a region whose very fountains murmur the warning words 'Drink and away!' " With his total command of Arabic and his profound knowledge of the Muslim world, he had expected the Consulate-General in Damascus, or at least Tangier. Instead he was shunted off to a place he considered a third-rate middle-class backwater on the edge of a hide-bound empire, where only the polyglot hubbub of the docks could speak to him of romance.

He hated the climate of Trieste, especially the bora (when it nearly blew his carriage sideways into the harbour one day he jumped out on the other side, leaving the driver to his fate). He was dispirited by its humdrum routines, which he relieved by teaching himself Russian and modern Greek and by translating pornographic literature from the Arabic. For years the Burtons lived in a large apartment near the Sudbahn railway station, up a flight of 120 stairs, but Richard liked eating out "to relieve the curse of domesticity." "We have formed a little 'mess,' " he reported in 1878, "with fifteen friends at the *table d'hôte* of the Hôtel de la Ville. . . . At dinner we hear the news, if any, take our coffee, cigarettes, and *kirsch* outside the hotel, then go homewards to read ourselves to sleep, and tomorrow *da capo*. . . ."

He says "we," but actually his wife Isabel was much more content in Trieste, which she characterized as "a dear old place." She loved him passionately, but he could embarrass her. Local society, which welcomed her, was wary of her Satanic husband. His fearful reputation had preceded him, and he did nothing to refute it. When Isabel once entertained a group of ladies at their apartment, and they wanted to see what the great man was writing just then, they found carefully disposed for their inspection a manuscript entitled *A History of Farting*.

And yet it was in Trieste that this difficult diplomat completed his greatest literary work, his translation of *The Thousand and One Nights,* with its famously improper supplementary notes. Wherever the Burtons lived in the world, Richard arranged a secluded retreat, well away from the crowds, far from the office, just in case (as Isabel put it) "he was feeling seedy." He was seedy for much of his time, now that he was in his late sixties, and the retreat he found was a set of rooms at a hostelry at Opicina, close to the Obelisk. This had been a posting inn, the last on the road from Vienna to Trieste, but by Burton's day it was chiefly used by weekenders escaping the summer heat below. Opicina remained, however, an essentially Slovene village of the Karst, more often spelt Občina, and so perhaps offered the superannuated adventurer some faint echoes of more haggard lands and wilder men. Here it was that he completed his masterpiece.

The inn is still there, but derelict, with swinging shutters and broken doors and overgrown terraces. Around the side of it, down a basement tunnel, there is a plaque on an inner wall with a relief of Sir Richard, and an inscription recording the improbable fact that in this building he opened the eyes of the western world to the full glory of the Arabian Nights. I like to loiter around the place, looking down to the wide blue bay beyond the city, hearing the distant buzz of its traffic and the whistle of the wind through the pines, and thinking of the formidable old exile labouring away inside, seedy, proud and resentful, while he wrote of the flying horses, the harems, the wizards and the Caliphs of his other world.

FOR MOST of its exiles Trieste was not a bad place to be, after all, if only because a web of fellow-feeling united you with your peers. Ex-kings bowed to discarded princes, landless aristocrats visited each other's salons, even Burton doubtless found himself a few congenial idiosyncrats. And James Joyce, reading a manuscript by the shy young businessman who wrote as Italo Svevo, recognised it at once as the work of a fellow-artist—living there in metaphorical banishment, like himself, among the clerks and the accountants.

EIGHT

One Night at the Risiera

But of course it was Jews that the passage of those trains along the waterfront always brought to my mind. Even now, when I see in memory's eye a last dingy wagon of the 1950s, trundling away towards the old fish market, I see too the lights of more dreadful trains disappearing into the eastern forests on their way to Auschwitz. In my mind Jews and Trieste go together, and the long and fruitful association of the two has made the city what it is—or at least, what it seems to me to be in those moments, ten minutes before the hour, when the idea of it bewitches me. In Habsburg times people in Vienna considered Trieste a Jewish city, and in a way I still do.

They say that you can take a Jew out of exile, but you can never take exile out of a Jew. Actually, for a hundred and fifty years the Jewish diaspora in Trieste was for the most part happy and successful. In many ways Jews did set the style of the place. They were encouraged to settle here from the first years of its Habsburgian expansion, under Maria Theresa. They had already proved their cosmopolitan value in the development of other European ports—Livorno, London, Hamburg, Amsterdam, Bordeaux: in this brand-new mercantile enterprise, on the edge of a continental empire, they would be especially useful. Generous privilege induced them to come: freedom from restrictions imposed upon Jews elsewhere in the empire, exemption from military service, guaranteed freedom of worship and investment. Rich and educated Jews were undoubtedly preferred.

The Trieste Jews formed an imperial category of their own, and they flourished mightily. If Italians, Germans, Englishmen, Slovenes and Croats provided maritime skills, and Greeks commercial know-how, it was above all Jews who built the financial structure of the new Trieste. They very soon became prominent in the Chamber of Commerce, and they dominated the insurance business, which was to be a main source of Trieste's wealth and influence. Jewish families formed part of the social elite—at the foot of the Old City there was a small walled ghetto with schools and synagogues, but most members of the community lived outside it, and fashionable Jewish houses were fashionable indeed.

Jews were prominent here as nowhere else in the empire. An extraordinary proportion of Trieste's artists and intellectuals were Jews or part Jews, often from business backgrounds—as early as 1797 Pope's *Essay on Man* was translated into Hebrew by Joseph Morpurgo, an insurance tycoon whose family name was to become a synonym for wealth in Trieste. Joyce had many Jewish friends in the city, and when he came to write *Ulysses*, which was inspired by Trieste almost as profoundly as it was by Dublin, he called it "an epic of two races." So powerful and prosperous did the Jewish community become, over the generations, that in 1912 it built for itself one of the biggest and most opulent synagogues in all Europe, magnificently positioned in the very heart of the city, around the corner from the Caffè San Marco—where many of its congregation were familiar customers, and which served kosher food for them.

This was the first synagogue I ever entered in my life. It was a splendid building, built so the guide-books say in the Syrian-Babylonian style, but more convincingly neo-Byzantine. It had a high central dome, castellated towers and a huge rose window in the form of David's star, and it was richly endowed with holy objects. Unlike so many other synagogues in Europe, it did not hide itself away unobtrusively, or try to look more or less like a private house. It was majestic and unmistakeable, and every passer-by knew it to be the proud temple of the Hebrews.

It was still very splendid when I diffidently strayed into it in 1946, still suggestively oriental beneath its high echoing dome. The occupying German army had closed it for a time and used it as a bullion deposit, but it was undamaged, and a chaplain of the Jewish Brigade of my own army had helped to officiate at its re-opening. Yet I sensed that it had lost its magic. Its fabric was decayed, its treasures were nowhere to be seen, and even its holiness seemed subdued. Presently I realized that there was a good reason for this. It was because almost all the Jews of Trieste, almost every one, had been driven away or murdered.

WHEN the bad times came in the 1930s, Trieste played an honourable role in helping the Jews of central Europe to escape their fate. There were then about five thousand Jews in the city. Zionism was strong here already, and the community (secretary, Carlo Morpurgo) formed a Committee of Assistance chiefly to get Jewish emigrants to Palestine. Train after train brought them in their thousands to the quays, where in the ships of Lloyd Triestino they sailed to the Promised Land in British-ruled Palestine, or at least to the Americas. Trieste acquired a further cognomen—the Port of Zion. A new little synagogue was established especially for transients, in the Via del Monte on the flank of San Giusto hill, and some of them went no further after all, but decided to stay in the city. Many more spent a few days or weeks here, awaiting a passage, and among them was Albert Einstein.

Most of Trieste's own Jews did not board the ships. Until 1938 they had not much reason to. The Fascist government in Rome did not trouble them, and all their institutions functioned: the hospital, the charitable societies, the infant schools, the rest home, the summer camp up at Opicina, the Fascist Youth Group . . . After 1938, when the Italians brought in racial laws of their own and the British clamped down on immigration into Palestine, the Trieste Jews could not leave even if they wanted to, and so it was that in 1943 history caught up with them. It was the fourth year of the second world war, and the Italians then turned against their German allies and signed an armistice with the western Powers. Instantly, the very next day, the Nazis took over Trieste. Several hundred Jews escaped into Italy, or to Switzerland. A few hid in Trieste for the rest of the war. Some seven hundred were called to death or deportation.

At San Sabba, where Joyce watched the scullers race, there is a former rice treatment plant, a bland enough place among the jumbled installations of the industrial port, wound about by elevated freeways. Trucks forever rumble by it, on their way to and from the piers. This banal group of buildings is where the Nazis committed the ultimate evil of Trieste. They used it as a police barracks, and then converted it into their only extermination camp in Italian soil—except that they did not regard Trieste as Italian territory, but declared it an integral part of the Reich. When I was first in Trieste the Risiera of San Sabba must have been far less obscured by industrial developments, but I never noticed it there and nobody ever mentioned it to me; yet in the previous two years hundreds of Jews had been exterminated there, and many more selected for deportation from which they never returned.

I hate to go there now. It is one place in Trieste that speaks of the tragic rather than the poignant. Although it is now an Italian national memorial and a tourist site, with its bare walls and shadows, its death chamber, its vile cells and the site of its crematorium, it still feels menacingly terrible to me. As it happens it stands not far from the city's Jewish cemetery, where in happier times Jews had passed to a more proper end. Going there in 1911 to the funeral of a friend, Joyce had seen its graves and tombstones with prophetic vision. "Corpses of Jews lie around me rotting in the mould of their holy field . . . black stone, silence without hope . . ."

THERE was a time when I used to say that if I were a Jew, I would certainly be a Zionist. I had soldiered in Palestine under the British Mandate, and had thought it was the Arabs, not the Jews, who were getting the raw deal there; but watching the young Israeli army storming through Sinai in the first of its wars fired me with romantic sympathy for the little State. Later I changed my mind again, and realized that the Jews I most admired were those Jews of the diaspora who had not abandoned their pride of origin, who were closely bound together by history and culture, by a love of words and music and debate, but who were essentially supra-national, extraterritorial citizens of the world. It is their spirit, diffused but inherent, like a gene in the chromosome, that makes me think of Trieste as a Jewish city still.

Jews are still around here, too. Their old ghetto, in the area behind the Piazza Unità, has mostly been destroyed in civic development, but what remains of it, as in many another former ghetto of Europe, has become rather trendy. Excellent bookstores, antiques shops, art dealers and picture restorers abound, and there is a Sunday flea market. On Via del Monte the transients' synagogue houses a Jewish museum, presided over by a rabbi from the Great Synagogue, and there is a Jewish school next door. Here and there, though, abandoned medieval lanes survive, awaiting demolition, and their tall shuttered empty houses, their lamps, chains, padlocks and stray cats, are reminders of more cruel times. Only the other day in the old ghetto area I saw three raggety buskers sent packing by the police, and as they packed up their cases, humped their instruments under their arms and trailed away towards the waterfront, I thought they looked very like poor Jews of long ago, being herded off to railway trucks.

I used to know a woman in this city who, by some accident of ill-fortune, had spent a single night in the Risiera at San Sabba. She told me that in retrospect that one night seemed as long as all the rest of her life put together, just as what happened to the Jews of Trieste in 1943 may well last longer in the collective memory than all their years of successful exile.

NINE

Borgello, Kofric, Slokovich and Blotz

"We are the eastern limit of Latinity and the southern extremity of Germanness," a Mayor of Trieste told me long ago. He might well have said that they were the western extremity of Slavdom, too, but perhaps that would then have been politically incorrect. Any Mayor of Trieste has to think ethnically, because this city is not simply a junction of political frontiers, it is an old fusion of bloodstocks. Today its population is overwhelmingly Italian, but I am told that when its football team goes to play in the Italian south, its players are still cat-called as Slavs or Balkans. Trieste is of Italy, but not altogether of it, and nothing could be much less like the effusive, song-singing, tricky, sun-burnt, fast-driving and volatile Italian of the world's imagination than your average Triestino.

A look at passing faces will confirm that. In the countryside around Trieste live many Slovenes of purest blood. Within the city are thousands of utter Italians. But for generations this place was a melting-pot of races and types, and its faces show it still. There is the straight northern Italian face, firm but a little dreamy; there is the Germanic Austrian face; there are faces with high cheek-bones and slightly slanting eyes that speak of

Hungary; there are fair-haired, blue-eyed Balkan faces. Very few of them are absolute, though. They are all mixed up, a tinge here, an echo there. The hybrid human is the norm in this city. Mayor Illy's paternal grandfather was from Transylvania; his grandmother was half-Irish and half-Austrian. Maestro Banfield-Tripcovich of the tugs and the Opera Verdi was the son of an Austrian of Irish descent, by a Slovene countess. Temperaments merge here too; Slataper the poet said of himself that blended in his character was Slavic nostalgia, German certainty and an Italian instinct for harmony.

Any list of Trieste names, in almost any context, is bewilderingly multi-ethnic. Take for instance a war memorial slab beneath the walls of the citadel, up on San Giusto hill. The most summary run of your eye down its roster will show you a Borgello, a Slocovich, a Brunner, a Sylvestro, a Zottin and a Blotz. The orchestra that played Smareglia's *Nozze Istriani,* last time I was at the opera, included violinists named Ivevic and Leszczynski, a cellist called Iztpk Kodric, Neri Noferini a horn player and an oboist named Giuseppi Mis Cipolat. Down the generations many Triestini have had their names ethnically adjusted, too, as a sort of first step towards genetic reconstruction. A Topico might become a Topić, a Kogut turn into a Cogetti. It depended upon the political circumstances of the day, and upon economic opportunity. Sometimes a change was made by order of the State, sometimes it was made as an explicitly personal statement. Italo Svevo, for instance, was born Ettore Schmitz: his *nom de plume* told everyone that he was Italian by loyalty but was born in Swabia, and combined in himself elements of both their cultures.

In all this Trieste was a microcosm of the empire. In a fractious moment Joyce once complained that the Dual Monarchy contained a hundred races speaking a thousand languages, and Mussolini thought its successor State of Czechoslovakia ought really to be called Czecho-Germano-Polono-Rutheno-Romano-Slovakia. In my library I have an Ethnographical Map of the Austro-Hungarian Empire, printed in Germany in 1896, which is a patchwork of faded multichrome blodges—pink for Germans, buff for Slovenes, dark green for Slovaks, light green for Poles, blue for Italians, mauve for Rhaeto-Romanes. I can't quite make out the colour of Trieste, but it looks sort of orangy.

WHAT is race? God knows. Even the word is ambiguous. Is a race ever the same as a nation? Can a nation be multi-racial? Can a race be defined by language? Can it be acquired? Does it depend upon colour? Is it affected by culture? How does patriotism apply to race? Can you feel truly patriotic for your place of residence, while feeling alien to its race? Or is patriotism really just racial pride? Suppose you are half-Italian and half-Slav, the most common cross in Trieste. Are you less Slovene if you don't speak Slovene? Are you more Italian if you support AC Milan? Whether racial characteristics are inherited or environmental, whether they are ineradicable or adjustable, whether they should be fostered or discouraged, admitted or denied, whether patriotism is racially innate or historically acquired—these are matters I often think about in this city.

I am myself a racial half-breed (father Welsh, mother English), and I have experienced some of the lesser quandaries of a condition that has been so common here. Many a Triestine dilemma has also been endemic in Wales, where problems caused by the arrival of the English nearly a thousand years ago have never been resolved. So many upwardly-mobile Slovenes of Trieste came to use Italian that it became as much a badge of class as of ethnicity, and similarly it was far more posh in Wales, until a few years ago, to speak English than Welsh. How many Joneses have become Iwans, how many Ifors spell their names Ivor, how many chapel-goers migrated to the Anglican Church, specifically to declare an allegiance or get on in the world? Some of my own children have preferred to spell their names in the old Welsh way, Morys, and I would do the same if I hadn't left it too late.

However there has been one fundamental difference between the Triestine and the Welsh circumstances. The native Welsh have resented the intrusion of the English not just on historical, linguistic or political grounds, but as a matter of instinct: they have disliked them as a people—the bloody *Saeson,* the Saxons. But for generations, it seems, problems of race did not disturb the Triestini. There was political antipathy between subjects and rulers, Italians against Austrians, perhaps religious prejudice too, but there appears to have been little purely ethnic bigotry. It does not arise in the Triestine literature I have read, and all the nineteenth-century travellers appear to have admired the easy inter-racial jumble of the place. There were entirely Slav quarters of town in those days, and nearby villages of the Karst were entirely Slovene in race as in language. Jews, Greeks, Serbs, Germans and British all had their own temples or churches. There were Armenians and Turks around. Yet one hears of no race riots or pogroms, senses no bigotries, and in 1908 the same man was choirmaster of the chief Jewish synagogue, the Greek Orthodox Church and the Serbian Orthodox Temple.

It was when the old empire collapsed that racial zealotry erupted. When the Italian government arrived in 1919, and wanted to make Trieste as Italian as possible, it banned all Slovene schools and turned a blind eye on violence against Slavs—the Balkan Hotel, the centre of Slav cultural life in the city, was burnt down by a mob with the connivance of the police. Conversely, when the Yugolavs arrived in 1945, and wanted to make the city entirely Yugoslav, they opened the Slovene schools again and obliged many Italians to change their names. There were violent race riots during the years of uncertainty, when nobody knew whether Trieste was to be Italian, Yugoslav or a Free City; in those times the world's predominant image of the place was of furious mobs, flying one banner or another, swarming through the Piazza Unità shouting ethnic slogans.

Today the question of race seems to have lost most of its bitter force. Black street vendors from the old Italian colonies of Africa are familiars of the town, pressing newspapers upon passers-by, sitting over their invariable collections of leather goods or wandering into the Caffè San Marco, muffled in scarves and balaclavas, to sell lottery tickets. Chinese entrepreneurs have acquired many of the shops of the *borgo teresiano,* identifiable by the paper lanterns that hang outside them, and offering motley stocks of clothes, knick-knacks and probably under-the-counter substances. And the still substantial Slovene minority, 8 percent of the whole, has its own schools and cultural centres, its daily newspaper and its theatre. The Slovene language has official parity with Italian, making this formally a bilingual city, and although there is no longer a specifically Slovene quarter of town, still the further you walk out towards the perimeter of the city, the more Slav it feels.

Of course inherited antipathies are not dead. Seventy-five years after the event hundreds of Slovenes attended a ceremony to remember the burning-down of the Balkan Hotel. Many of the Italians who came here as dispossessed refugees from Istria, when the Yugoslav Croatians and Slovenes took over the peninsula in 1954, cherish an ineradicable resentment against all Slavs, just as so many of the French *colons* driven out of Algeria can never forgive an Arab. I am told there is latent anti-Slav feeling, too, among older citizens in general. When the laws guaranteeing equality of language were instituted I stumbled upon a neo-Fascist meeting of protest, and very unpleasant it was: to raucous music and fluttering flags a strutting demagogue shouted hatred into a loud-hailer—biligualism, he screamed, meant there was no future for Italians in Trieste, no jobs, no hope, and his skin-head lieutenants, in long shorts and running-shoes, offered inflammatory leaflets to passers-by.

They found few takers, though. It seems to me that such popular prejudice as there is in Trieste nowadays is much more diffuse. A rabbi told me once that although he did occasionally feel tremors of anti-semitism, he believed it to be only a symptom of a vague general suspicion of difference—"if I didn't wear this hat and this beard, I'd probably never sense it." The chief resentment I myself detect is directed against the flood of new settlers from southern Italy, on the grounds that they are changing the character of the city with their noise, bad manners and disorderly conduct.

For half a century now Trieste has been politically relaxed, and the vicious racism of the twentieth century has faded like a bora blown out. The later Cold War generally ignored Trieste. The wars of Yugoslav succession passed it by. Economically it no longer matters much whether you are Slovene or Italian by origin, especially as by now the chances are that you are a mixture of both, with perhaps some Austrian or Jewish thrown in, or an American or British gene left by a transient soldier long ago. I noticed the same at home in Wales—that when people felt they were achieving some degree of national fulfilment, racial bitterness subsided. Even that most intractable kind of racial antipathy, the mutual fear and distaste between people of different colour, fades when political and economic circumstances are the same for both sides. Could it be that racism is a sort of historical invention, a Satanic hoax?

Trieste remains, nonetheless, an ethnic enclave of sorts. It first became part of an Italian State as the result of a secret agreement during the first world war, when Italy was induced to join the western allies by the promise of Trieste, Istria and the Italian town of Zara, now Zadar, on the Dalmatian coast. Istria and Zara were transferred to Yugoslavia after the second world war, and if racial logic had then prevailed Trieste would not now be an Italian city either, but the port of Slovenia—Trst. The natural ethnic frontier (if one is to go by language, the only acceptably measurable standard) ran well to the west, half-way to Venice—the final eastern line between the Habsburg empire and the kingdom of Italy. Trieste was just a predominantly Italian-speaking city in a Slav territory, no more anomalous in its setting than the heavily German city of Riga in Latvia or the Polish Vilnius in Lithuania, both alien urban centres with an indigenous peasantry all around. As it was, Yugoslavia was obliged to spend vast sums of money developing the port of Rijeka, formerly Fiume; and when Yugoslavia disintegrated, half a century later, Slovenia had to develop its own outlet to the sea—the port of Koper, *quondam* Capodistria, only just out of sight from Trieste itself.

REMEMBER that war memorial, up on the hill of San Giusto, with such an enigmatic variety of names upon it? I puzzled over that slab when I first went to Trieste because it claimed to honour the dead of the first world war, but neglected to say which country they had died for. Here, evidently, race and patriotism did not always go together. The father of that honoured Italian citizen Baron de Banfield-Tripcovich was a hero of the Austrian air force, fighting against the Italians in the first world war. He was called "The Eagle of Trieste," and was ennobled as Baron of Trieste by the Dual Monarchy, but when the war ended and Trieste became Italian he was imprisoned as a traitor. There are still ancients in Trieste who parade with their medals and banners as veterans of Franz Joseph's armed forces—I went to a church service of theirs once, and their solemnity and stately moustaches would have done credit to the *lamparetti*. On the Karst live many old soldiers who fought with the Yugoslav partisans in the second world war, and who carefully tend the village war memorials, still with the star of Communism on them, that remember once irreconcilable enemies of Italy. There are people in this city whose grandparents were born Austrian, whose parents came into the world as Italians, who were themselves born as citizens of a Free Territory and whose children are Italian again. A few miles away, just across the border, aged citizens have been governed in their own lifetimes by Austrians, Italians, Germans, Britons, Yugoslavs and Slovenians.

I thought it very odd, when I was young, and encountered the Trieste mélange of loyalties. I was a simple British patriot in those days—even Wales was subsumed in my idea of a benevolent and majestic British nation-state, benign suzerain of an unexampled empire, headed by a monarch everyone respected, led at that time by a charismatic champion, victorious as ever and destined to live happily ever after. I was not in the least chauvinistic; in fact I was everyone's patriot, as easily moved by "La Marseillaise" or even "Deutschland Über Alles" as I was by "God Save the King." I assumed that my contemporaries' patriotism was as liberal as my own, only becoming suspect when it descended into the obdurate banality of "My country right or wrong." In short my views were probably much like those of most Britons of my age and kind, at the end of the second world war.

No wonder I was taken aback by the muddled fealties of Trieste! There were Italians here then who were still proud of their Fascist State, or who were altogether disillusioned by it. There were Communist Slovenes who boasted of their new People's Federation, and royalist Croats who utterly disowned it, and separatists who thought in terms of Slovenia, Croatia, Serbia, Bosnia or Herzegovina, entities I hardly knew existed. There were old ladies forever recalling the lost glories of *K u K* in Trieste, and sure that nothing could ever replace them. When I realized that all these contradictory loyalties were perfectly genuine—when I worked out the meaning of those names on the war memorial—I began to see the idea of the nation-state in a new light. I already knew Dr. Johnson's saw, about patriotism being the last refuge of the scoundrel. Now I glimpsed the fateful nonsense of nationalism, for which so many of my generation, and my father's too, had fought and died.

TEN

The Nonsense of Nationality

One warm day in 1946 I sat down on a bollard on the Molo Audace, close to the Piazza Unità, to write a maudlin essay. The Yanks, Brits and Jugs (as we called each other then) still disputed the city, and Trieste was of no decided country, no particular allegiance, no certain ideology. The successor to its Austrian Governors and Italian Prefects was an American general, and up on the Karst Tito's commissars held sway. British and American military officers did the work of the imperial and Fascist bureaucrats. The Royal Navy provided a Port Captain. The Hôtel de la Ville was the American officers' club, the Albergo Savoia Excelsior was ours, and where the soldiers of the Austrian 18th Infantry Division had sauntered, or the plumed *bersaglieri* swaggered, there was I, sitting on the jetty writing an essay.

It was a piece about nostalgia, but nostalgia for a place and condition I had never known: Europe before the convulsions of the twentieth century had upset all its assumptions. I had never been to continental Europe before the war, so my nostalgia was all hearsay, but was none the less pungent for that. I pined for a Europe that seemed in my fancy to form a cohesive whole, sharing values and manners and aspirations, and when I looked around me at the Trieste of 1946, I thought I could see the ghost of that ideal. Except for its docks the city had not been greatly damaged, and its buildings still offered an epitome of Mitteleuropa—of Europe distilled, as it were. It seemed to embody the very mixture of races and languages, the civilized continuity of culture, that I imagined for my lost continent as a whole. Students and artists still frequented its coffee-houses. Bookshops abounded. Wine flowed. A Smareglia opera was being performed in the opera house that very season, just as one had been performed there (so a programme note told me) in 1885, 1886, 1895, 1899, 1900, 1908, 1910, 1921, 1926, 1928, 1929 and 1930. Ships came and went, as they came and went from Hamburg and Marseilles, Oslo and the Piraeus. Steam trains laboured along the waterfront, as I imagined them criss-crossing European landscapes from Scotland to the Alps. So I sat there on my bollard like a figure in an allegory, sucking my pen and cogitating, and thinking up poignant adjectives.

But I was deluded, of course, in my nostalgia. The Europe of my dreams had never existed, above all because of nationality. If race is a fraud, as I often think in Trieste, then nationality is a cruel pretence. There is nothing organic to it. As the tangled history of this place shows, it is disposable. You can change your nationality by the stroke of a notary's pen; you can enjoy two nationalities at the same time or find your nationality altered for you, overnight, by statesmen far away. In one of his books Joseph Conrad (né Korzeniowski), knowing how artificial nationality was, likened it to "an accomplishment with varying degrees of excellence." It is not usually racial prejudice that incites hooligans to bash each other in football stadiums, but particularly unaccomplished convictions of nationhood. The false passion of the nation-state made my conceptual Europe no more than a chimera: and because of nationality the city around me that day, far from being a member of some mighty ideal whole, was debilitated in loneliness.

NATIONALISM flared in Trieste when, during the nineteenth century, most of Italy became united in the passionate progression of the Risorgimento, and the kingdom of Italy under King Vittore Emanuele II came into being. It was not only an Italian movement. The libertarian risings of the 1840s happened all over the Habsburg possessions—one of Musil's characters called them "all this tuppeny-halfpenny liberty-mongering of the Czechs and the Poles and the Italians and the Germans." But the Italians set the pace of it, and by the 1870s Trieste remained the one foreign-held city that Italian nationalists claimed as their own. The new Italian frontier was only a few miles from Trieste, and regions that had long been under the city's jurisdiction were now in a foreign country. But was it foreign? More and more Italians of Trieste did not think so. They found themselves caught in Garibaldi's spell, and a word entered the political vocabulary that was specifically related to their city: *irredentismo,* irredentism, the condition of being un-redeemed. For thousands of Triestini it became a battle-cry, and the complacent nature of Trieste changed.

Now the political police had their hands full, and the *lamparetti* were kept busy chasing slogan-scrawlers and statue-chippers. Secret societies were formed; explosives were stashed; many of the cafés, so comfortably reminiscent of Old

Vienna, became hotbeds of Italian dissent. All came to a head in 1882 when an exhibition was held in the city to celebrate the five hundredth anniversary of Habsburg Trieste, and it was announced that the Emperor himself would be visiting it. A young Triestine named Guglielmo Oberdan (originally, as it happened, Oberdank), who had fled to Italy to avoid serving in the Austrian army, returned to Trieste with two bombs and a revolver in his suitcase, and his mind on assassination. The authorities were waiting for him. He was arrested, tried for treason and hanged in the Austrian barracks of the city, crying to the end "Viva Italia! Viva Trieste Libera!"

So the irredentists of Trieste gained a martyr, and they used him well. Their cause boomed. The Italians of the city became ever more estranged from the Austrians, and vice versa. Few young Italians would go near the Caffè Eden, the favourite resort of Austrian officials; not many Austrians would venture into the hotly irredentist Caffè San Marco. Isabel Burton wrote that an Austrian would hardly give his hand to an Italian at a dance, and no Italian would attend a concert when an Austrian was singing. If Austrians gave a party Italians threw a bomb into it, she said, and members of the imperial family were greeted with "a chorus of bombs, bombs on the railway, bombs in the garden, bombs in the sausages." A *lodogno* tree outside the doors of the cathedral, survivor of an ancient cemetery there, was adopted as an ostentatiously sacred symbol of Italianness, and the imperial secret police became ubiquitous—even transient visitors with the slightest claim to nationalist sympathies found themselves under surveillance.

When the Austrians proposed to erect a statue of the Emperor in the Piazza Giovanni, Italian patriots forestalled them with a marble figure of Verdi, and everyone knew what that signified—Verdi was Trieste's most popular composer not simply because of his associations with the city, but also because *Nabucco* was the symbolic opera of the Risorgimento, and because the letters of the composer's name had become an acronym of irredentist loyalty, standing for **V**ittore **E**manuele **R**e **D**'**I**talia. On the birthday of the King of Italy almost every Italian in Trieste wore a flower in his button-hole; on the birthday of the Emperor the only flags that flew were on the Governor's palace, the barracks and the prison. The day after the assassination of King Umberto of Italy, in 1900, patrolling *lamparetti* found the cherub Giovannini del Ponterosso dressed in full mourning. The only statue of the Emperor in the entire city was inside the main post office—the one precluded by Verdi in the Piazza Giovanni; sadly disillusioned by his Most Faithful City, Franz Joseph never went near the place during the last twenty years of his life.

Within Italy not everyone was much interested in Trieste: even the great Risorgimentist Giuseppe Mazzini had not claimed it for his State. In 1882 the Italian Kingdom itself, having got most of what it wanted from the Habsburg empire, seemed to abandon the city by concluding an alliance with Austria. But when the Archduke Ferdinand was assassinated at Sarajevo in 1914 the Trieste *italianissimi* saw his killer as a reincarnation of Oberdan, and the consequent world war as a vehicle of redemption; and sure enough two years later the Italians switched alliances and declared war on Austria. In Trieste irredentism in all its aspects became treasonable, and what remained of the old civic equilibrium was shattered. The newspaper *Il Piccolo,* which represented all that was most Italian in the city, was summarily closed down. The Caffè San Marco was burnt out. The Verdi statue was destroyed. The sacred tree of San Giusto was dug up and replaced by one less full of meaning.

The Italians fought their war on battlefields that were often within earshot of Trieste, and under the peace treaty of Rapallo they were given their prize. The Risorgimento was completed; Trieste was redeemed. On November 3, 1918, when the Austrian administration was still functioning in the city, the destroyer *Audace* (1,017 tons) sailed in from Venice carrying a contingent of *bersaglieri,* the first troops of the Kingdom of Italy to set foot in Trieste. Watched by an exultant crowd the ship tied up at the Molo San Carlo, close to the Piazza Grande. The name of this pier commemorated both an eponymous Austrian warship that had sunk there long before, and the Austrian Emperor Charles VI who had first established the greatness of Trieste. The jubilant Italians immediately renamed it after the little warship of their success, and it has been the Molo Audace ever since.

O, THE ORGY of triumphalism that ensued, the re-naming of streets and bars and cafés, the adjustments of allusion, the revisions of loyalty! Riva Carciotti became Riva 3 Novembre. Molo Giuseppino became Molo Bersaglieri. Piazza Grande became Piazza dell'Unità d'Italia. The Caffè Flora became the Caffè Nazionale. The Porto Nuovo, which had become the Porto Vecchio, became the Porto Vittorio Emanuele III. The Verdi statue was replaced with a replica, made by its original sculptor from the metal of captured Austrian guns. From here, the City of Redemption, the vulgarly romantic adventurer Gabriele D'Annunzio set off with his private army of filibusters, in cloaks, daggers and feathered hats, to seize Fiume for Italy too. And when the Fascists came to power in 1922 they cherished Trieste as a supreme national and even expansionist symbol. It was Roman. It was Italian. It was theirs by right of history and conquest, and the centuries of Habsburg rule had been no more than an interlude. Besides, as an official publication declared, "The Fascist Government is profoundly cognizant of the importance of Trieste for the economic and political expansion of Italy in the Central Danube hinterlands."

IN FACT Trieste became just another provincial Italian city with an uncertain future, and it soon lost its old allure—James Joyce, who returned for a few months after the war, was soon disillusioned by it, and went away for good. But the Fascists adopted it as their own, and made it one of their show-places. Oberdan became, in retrospect, a Fascist as well as an irredentist hero, and his memory was carefully fostered. The Piazza Caserma was renamed Piazza Oberdan in his honour, and on the site of the barracks where he was executed a Museum of the Risorgimento was opened. It is still there, and inside it is reverently preserved the cell where Oberdan spent the last days of his life, as St. Francis's woodland hut and Lincoln's log cabin have been reconstructed by cultists of other kinds. In a sort of dark shrine nearby, on the exact spot of his death, a gaunt statue of the martyr is guarded by weeping angels with intersecting wings, rather as brides are attended with crossed swords at military weddings.

Mussolini's men in Trieste were headed by a Prefect, installed in the palace of the Austrian Governors. Their first ideological purpose was to establish the ancient Italianness of the place, and remind everyone that it had been a Roman colony long before Austria had ever been heard of. Scholars quoted Dante to demonstrate that Istria, beyond Trieste, had always been the easternmost territory of Italy. Archaeologists restored the Roman amphitheatre that we glimpsed on our first day in town: in a 1930s picture of it that I have before me now a placard proclaims hugely from a nearby wall "ROMA DOMA"—which I take to signify "Rome Rules, OK?" They restored the Roman forum on the hill above, too, built a Via Capitolina up to to it and liked to recall that until the nineteenth century the hill had been popularly known as Monte Tiber. They erected a heroically Italian war memorial up there, all shields, naked torsos and fasces; they erected a catafalque commemorating the victorious Italian Third Army of the first world war, decorated with a machine-gun, a bomb, a shell, a howitzer and a dagger, together with a map marking the Mediterranean as Mare Nostrum; they carefully preserved the *lodogno* tree by the cathedral door.

At the top of the Scala dei Giganti, the grandest of the city's stone staircases, an immense column was erected, with a fountain playing around it, to provide the city centre with the kind of declamatory ensemble both Romans and Fascists loved. A university was opened, with a histrionic headquarters on the edge of town, and official structures of one sort and another went up opposite the amphitheatre. A start was made on a trunk road to link the centre of Trieste with the Italian national highway system. The upper part of the Canal Grande was filled in for the sake of traffic improvements. A handsome new Maritime Station, for long-haul passenger traffic, was built on the Molo Bersaglieri. The Duke of Aosta moved into Miramare, as commander of the local air forces, and refurnished his quarters in what was described as the Rationalist manner. And on the slopes of the northern bay, overlooking the whole city, there appeared in 1927 a monumental lighthouse. Fifty years before, this would have been supported by emblematic images of Virtue, Prosperity or even Profit: now an alarmingly androgynous figure of Victory crowned it, winged and helmeted, and to its base was affixed the anchor of the *Audace*.

More than all this, the Fascists brought Fascism to Trieste. This is an innately conservative city, where politicians of the Right have generally been successful, and it welcomed Mussolini's messages. Across the city party symbols appeared, dates according to the Fascist era, buildings in the Fascist style. Within the port administration, once so proudly autonomous, a man from the Ministry of Communications in Rome could veto anything that might "compromise the interests of the State or not correspond to the government's political directives." Most of the city's Austrians had willy-nilly left, but now for the first time its Slavs found themselves second-class citizens. Many Croats and Slovenes preferred to leave too, for the new kingdom of Yugoslavia; those who remained were made to feel decidedly uncomfortable. Slovene schools and newspapers were banned; use of the Slovene language was prohibited "in any public situation." John Berger tells us (in his novel *G*, 1972), that when an Italian doctor was asked how patients could describe their symptoms to him if they didn't know Italian, he replied that a cow didn't have to explain its symptoms to a vet. . . .

This was nationalism—patriotism gone feral. The Trieste newspapers, once trenchantly outspoken, did not oppose the creeping advance of totalitarianism, and when in 1938 Mussolini himself visited the city to open new dock extensions and lay the keel of the battleship *Roma* (42,000 tons), the public celebrations were spectacular and unopposed. Vast panoplies of flags and banners were hoisted across the city, enormously embroidered with the word "DUCE," or just with the letter "M" in the Napoleonic manner. "DUCE DUCE DUCE DUCE," simply said the front-page streamer headline in the now sycophantic *Il Piccolo.* Uniformed functionaries by the thousand, formidable or ridiculous, fat or weedy, paraded here and there in jackboots and tasselled hats, swelling out their chests. The Fountain of the Four Continents was moved to allow a greater welcoming crowd to assemble in the Piazza Unità (which is why it was being moved back again sixty-two years later, when I happened to be passing by that day), and when the time came the biggest audience Trieste had ever known packed the brilliantly illuminated square to hear the dictator speak. He slept only two nights in the city, but sixty years later an entire book was devoted to his visit.

It was mostly bluff and blunder. This city was not economically vital to the Italians, as it had been to the Dual Monarchy—they had several other ports all much nearer their centres of trade and production. Its industries were important enough, especially its shipyards, but for the most part its possession was a matter of nationalist symbolism. "You should have been here in the Fascist times," said an Italian acquaintance of mine in 1946. "What a city it was then! You should have seen Mussolini in the Piazza!" But Trieste's Fascist years (Anno I–Anno XXI) did the city little good, and for all their braggadocio never revived its prosperity, or restored it to its place in the world at large.

WORSE was to come, anyway, in the varied causes of nationalism. In the second war, Italy having changed sides again, Trieste and its neighbouring coast was annexed by the Germans. It was called the Küstenland once more, and governed by a Gauleiter, until in 1945 two armies arrived almost simultaneously and threw the Germans out. From the west came a New Zealand division, with British armour. From the east came Marshal Tito's Yugoslav partisan forces, advance warning of the huge Communist power-bloc then coming into being. The Yugoslavs arrived first, but the Germans, their last troops by then shut up in the citadel on San Giusto hill, would surrender only to the New Zealanders: when they did, a stand-off ensued between the two victorious forces, who found themselves not allies-in-arms after all, but ideological enemies.

For a few years Trieste once more entered the world's consciousness, as the Powers argued what to do with it. No longer one of the supreme ports of Europe, it became instead one of those places, like Danzig or Tangier, that have been argued about at international conferences, written about in pamphlets, questioned about in parliamentary debates, less as living cities than as political hypotheses. Winston Churchill, in a famous speech in America, warned the world that an iron curtain had been laid across Europe, dividing democracy and Communism "from Stettin to Trieste." Abroad the statesmen endlessly parleyed; at home the Triestini of different loyalties, chanting slogans and waving their respective flags, surged about the place rioting.

Finally in 1954 the disconsolate and bewildered seaport was given its solution, and Trieste has been what it has been ever since, a geographical and historical anomaly, Italian by sovereignty but in temperament more or less alone.

MY COUNTRY right or wrong." How meaningless how it sounds nowadays, how preposterous! It is the slogan of blind nationalism. Patriotism, the love of one's people or one's country, seems to me still a noble emotion, but to my mind nationalism has come to mean no more than narrow and offensive chauvinism, based on baloney. Today you can qualify to play for the rugby team of a nation if just one of your grandparents happened to be born there, even if you have never been to the place, even if you speak no word of its language—a qualification almost as absurd as Nazi definitions of Jewishness. One day the very idea of nationality will seem as impossibly primitive as dynastic warfare or the divine right of kings; first the unification of continents, then the global rule of the almighty corporations, like institutions from space, then perhaps space itself and finally plain common-sense will reduce it to a hobby for antiquarians or re-enactment societies.

In Trieste more than anywhere the idea of nationality seems alien. The city was given its character by people from a dozen countries long ago, and is still innately solitary. It is by definition a city of the world, and I like to think it instinctively honours the playwright Saunders Lewis's Welsh criterion of true patriotism: *ysbrid hael ac o gariad at wareiddiad a thraddodiad a phethau gorau dynoliaeth*—"a generous spirit of love for civilization and tradition and the best things of mankind." Nationalist brags, envies or resentments do not become this city, and seldom surface here now: when a parade bursts out in the Piazza Unità, as it often does, with intoxicating displays of Italianism, feathered hats, formation flying, military bands and warships at the quay, the citizenry responds to a great show with happy and humorous enthusiasm, but never I think with the blind conformity that greeted Mussolini in Anno XVI. A civic publicity brochure I picked up in A.D. 2000 makes no reference to nationality at all—innocent readers would not know what country the city was in, since it is simply characterized as "one of the most interesting areas in Europe." I was encouraged, too, by a graffito I saw recently on a rubbish disposal bin in the Old City. "FUK NATIONS," it simply said.

During my original time in Trieste I had a dear friend who was to become central to my conception of the place. Otto was a bit of a mystery. His national origins were indeterminate. He had fought bravely on our side during the war that had just ended, yet he had briefly attended the Potsdam Military Academy, and he had elderly relatives in Vienna who allowed us to spend weekends in a princely apartment there. His English was curiously thickened. He stuttered. His manner was a mixture of the florid, the stiff and the deliberately outrageous. I believe he was in some way connected to the archetypal nineteenth-century adventurer Rudolf von Slatin, author of *With Fire and Sword Through the Sudan,* a title he loved resonantly quoting. Perhaps he was partly Jewish.

I used to tell this complex and delightful man that he was just made for inclusion in that inscrutably multi-ethnic memorial on San Giusto hill. In those days I thought of his ironically tolerant outlook as idiosyncratic cosmopolitanism, but now I would characterize it as Triesticity.

ELEVEN

Love and Lust

Italo Svevo, who was born in 1861 and died in 1928, seemed to live a prosaic life in Trieste, first as an insurance clerk, then as an executive in the family paint and varnish factory. If we are to believe his novels, though, behind the bourgeois façade of the city seethed all manner of sexual passion, as it did behind the rectitude of Victorian Britain: in one book the narrator is so addled by his own addictions and jealousies that he is giving himself a course of self-analysis, in another the city itself is interpreted as a tortuous paradigm of an infatuation.

Freud's ideas indeed found a ready audience among the Trieste intelligentsia, confused as they must have been even then by the ambivalence of the city, its ethnic muddles and historical complexities—as Scipio Slataper wrote at the turn of the twentieth century, "everything in Trieste is double or triple." I am confused here too, and have never felt more inclined to Freudian introspection than I am when idling the hours away in Trieste, contemplating the varied meanings of love and lust.

. . .

TAKE love first. The prime Trieste love story concerns Isabel Burton and her husband Richard, that irrepressible literary pornographer and investigator of sex. Lady Burton was a devout Catholic, and although she was permanently besotted by loving admiration for her husband, and had followed him through many of his desperate adventures, she was understandably uncomfortable with his alternative tastes and interests. After his death in Trieste she determined to obliterate a last trace of them. By then the couple had moved to an apartment in the splendid Palladian villa built by the Englishman George Hepburn 170 years before, and to this day one of the city's best buildings. Some days after the Consul's death, nosy passers-by looking through a window might have seen a bright fire burning in a bedroom grate, and Isabel passionately throwing papers into it—as though an enemy were at the gates, and she must destroy the consulate documents. In fact she was putting to the flames the two manuscript volumes of his unfinished final translation of *The Scented Garden,* said to be one of the most sensuously beautiful of all Arabic poems, with a commentary of his own rich in sexual scholarship. Burton himself said the book would be the crown of his life, but Isabel thought she could hardly do less than burn it, for the sake of Richard's soul and reputation.

She knew very well what she was doing. She knew she would sacrifice many friendships, and infuriate the literary world, and so it proved. Algernon Swinburne, an old friend, was plainly thinking of her when he wrote, in a long poetic elegy for Burton, that

> . . . Souls there are that for soul's afright
> Bow down and cower in the sun's glad sight,

Clothed round with faith that is one with fear,
And dark with doubt of the live world's light.

Another friend, the writer Ouida, never spoke to her again, and she was plagued by anonymous letters of abuse. But what she did, she did for love. It used to be said that she burnt the manuscript not in a bedroom grate, but in a bonfire in the garden of their house, and this is the version I prefer. The house is still there, although hemmed around by new apartment buildings, and I like to go up there in the evening and imagine the fire still ablaze beneath the trees behind—the crackle of the flames, the curling of the scorched pages one by one, and a trembling Isabel kneeling there, silhouetted against the light and muttering a prayer as she threw them into oblivion. How sad that her bonfire that night, which she saw as a beacon of truest dedication, should have been interpreted ever since as a conflagration of betrayal.

LUST is a different matter. I don't believe Burton was a particularly lustful man, his interest in the wide reaches of sex being mostly anthropological, or artistic. But down the hill from his house that night, lustful appetites were undoubtedly being indulged. As a great cosmopolitan seaport, Trieste in his time had a lively red-light quarter. Proust's Narrator, who had imagined it as deliciously melancholy, changed his mind when he heard that his Albertine was enjoying Sapphic sex there, and called it an accursed city that ought to go up in flames. The centre of low life was the area around the Piazza Cavana, at the back of the Piazza Unità at the foot of the Old City. Today it is a good place for secondhand bookshops, antiques and food stores, and only a few leprous alleys resist the scours of progress. A century ago, by all accounts, its mesh of little streets was stinking, crumbling, mouldy and permanently puddled. In those days ships docked a few blocks away, and this was where the seamen caroused, the soldiers came down from their barracks and the brothels flourished. The *lamparetti* knew it well. Saba often picked his way through its roistering crowds on his way home in the evening, feeling that the more squalid his route, the purer his thoughts.

Prostitution was legal in Italy until 1958, some of the brothels being State-owned. It thrives in Trieste still, but there is no red-light district now; business is dispersed more discreetly across the city, arranged by mobile telephones and concluded in private houses. It was to one of the old-style places of pleasure, though, that at his own request I once escorted a fellow-officer. He was no older than I was, had never been to such a place before, and was nervous. I dropped him at the doorstep of the brothel—could it have been the famous Oriental House?—and remember still how pale he stood there in the street-light, looking back at me almost desperately as I drove my jeep away into the night.

I have often wondered how he got on. A shy, well-scrubbed young man, born to the English countryside, how easily did he adapt to the ornate opulence of the place, somewhat akin as I imagine it to the décor of Baron Revoltella's mansion? His chief passion was steeple-chasing. Was he not repelled by the stuffy smells inside, of scent, cheap powder and cigarettes? Was his need really so urgent that he could disregard it all, and plunge himself, eyes closed and thinking of Becher's Brook, into such sleazy sublimation?

James Joyce is said to have been an assiduous drunken frequenter of the Trieste whore-houses, allegedly preferring *La Chiave d'Oro,* the Golden Key, or the poky *Il Metro Cubo,* the Cubic Metre. Drunken he certainly was, often having to be taken home by his brother Stanislaus, and very unlikely to be chaste. It was in Trieste that he wrote *A Portrait of the Artist as a Young Man,* a searing record of repentance after lustful sin, and he must have known what he was talking about. How strange it is nevertheless, that the man who wrote "Watching the Needle-Boats at San Sabba" in the daytime could stagger sozzled from pub to prostitute at night! Joyce adored his children and loved his wife after his fashion, yet apparently he still felt the need to wander, night after night, down the Via del Solitario to the House of the Golden Key.

I am of the opinion that lust is one of the more banal impulses, essentially functional and familiar not just to the birds and the diligent bees, but to any old lop-eared tomcat. In Trieste I ponder the mystery of its power over the most fastidious of point-to-point riders, or the very greatest of geniuses.

LOVE generally supersedes lust as we grow older, and nowadays a more amorphous kind of eroticism seizes me in this city. It is a sensuality of homesickness. I have always been homesick on my travels, missing my own people, my animals, my books, my house, my country, but somehow in Trieste it becomes homesickness of a wider range. It gives me a yearning pleasure when I telephone Wales before I go to sleep, and hear the beloved voices of home wishing me goodnight; yet it is a yearning that goes beyond them, to make me long for some even greater loving whole. There is something libidinous to this feeling, like the lusting of nuns for their God. Is it a latent religious instinct, or just the fathomless expectancy of Trieste, which always makes me look for something grander yet to come? Perhaps everyone feels it, in this city of hiatus. Perhaps my anxious subaltern, waiting on the doorstep, felt that he too was moving towards some more universal fulfilment, and Joyce knew that his whore's bed was a bed of Heaven after all, even if he had to be carried insensible home from it.

Certainly I sometimes think that transient love, the sort that is embodied in a one-night passion, or even a passing glance, is no less real than the lifelong sort. Even imagined love is true! It all comes from, and goes back to, the same illimitable reservoir that lies somewhere beyond my bedside telephone. Of course this foggy fancy suits my idea of Trieste. This is a place of transience, where power and prosperity come and go, and even the stateliest palaces of State or commerce seem insubstantial when you are in the mood. It makes me more than usually vulnerable to momentary consolations. The sight of a ship hull-down on the horizon—a sudden vision of the Dolomite snow-peaks—a cheerful gesture from a traffic-cop —a scrawny white cat looking up at me proudly as she chases her kitten to safety off the street—all such trifling incidents, in Trieste, sentimentally comfort me.

Long ago I was going out through the door of the Albergo Savoia Excelsior when a man simultaneously entered. We bumped into one another, our bags and luggage got mixed up, and we both apologized. He was a theatrical-looking character, with a camel coat slung over his shoulders—perhaps one of the opera singers from the Teatro Verdi, who habitually stay in the hotel. When we had disentangled ourselves he stood there for a moment motionless.

"Where are you from?" he said.

"Wales."

"Wales! How *wonderful!*"

Oh you splendid liar, I thought to myself, you've never heard of the place. There was a pause. I laughed, and so did he. He shook my hand in both of his, we lingered for a moment and parted. When I think of Trieste, love and lust, I often think of him.

TWELVE

The Wild Side

One evening I heard music in the street, and looking out of my window I saw two strange figures passing. One was a young man in a tall brown hat, blowing on a shepherd's flute. The other was attached by complex apparatus to a variety of apparently home-made instruments—bagpipes, drums, cymbals, a triangle I think—and in order to beat the biggest drum he had to move in an abrupt but creaky shuffle. Slowly and sporadically these engaging characters pottered down the pavement below me, tootling and drumming as they went.

In Trieste that day they were like visitors from another, less inhibited world. They brought a touch of the maverick to this ordered city. They were musicians from the Karst, strollers from the wild side.

EVERY great city, in my view, needs some element of disorder, or at least of the eccentric or the atavistic, to temper its arrangements. I mean dis-order as against un-order, as being dis-interested differs from being un-interested. Venice has its lagoon of floods and mudflats. Edinburgh has its grim Old

Town on the hill, permanently sneering at the Georgian urbanity below. Until recently Hong Kong had its notorious Walled City, a cloistered labyrinth whose very sovereignty was indeterminate. Most old cities have pockets of sin, where cautious visitors do not care to go, and it is a weakness of planned capitals that generations must pass before any of their districts acquire disreputable qualifications.

When the conscientious enthusiasts from Vienna first mapped out the New City of Trieste, they made no provisions for such districts either—no back-alleys or cul-de-sacs suitable for mayhem—but the gods of disorder have always been present here. Claudio Magris has pointed out that in the Public Garden, among all those honoured busts, hens and chickens have gone more or less feral, and scrabble about in the shrubberies like wild birds. He wonders if this portends similar regressions among other domestic species, but when I stand by the garden railings and watch them there, returned to the habits of their ancestral forests, I prefer to suppose they represent an instinct in the city itself to do the same.

I have seldom seen disorderly conduct in contemporary Trieste, but Paul Theroux witnessed a brawl on his second night in town, a perhaps invigorating surprise for him—he had thought Trieste the quietest and most law-abiding city of his Mediterranean travels. *Il Piccolo* does often report skullduggeries. Ironically the *borgo teresiano,* pride of the Akademie der Bildenden Künste, crops up in these dispatches most often, in connection with drugs, prostitution, Chinese feuds or illegal immigants—*clandestini;* but all I have myself uncovered, when I have poked around those shops with the paper lanterns, is an uncomfortable sensation that I am asking too many questions. One morning I read of a murder on the other side of town, near the industrial port. I went there at once, but my haul of misbehaviour was sparse there too: a few drunks, some obscene graffiti, and a mad woman who swore at me in the street ("Don't be scared," a passer-by reassured me, "I've known her for years, she swears at everybody"—and indeed, when in my discomfiture I dropped the jumper I was carrying, the lunatic hastened to return it to me with elaborate courtesy).

Of course war and politics have often brought atavism to Trieste. Irredentism introduced its undercurrent of delinquency to Urbs Fidelissima, and other peoples' conflicts have repeatedly alerted this peaceable place to the parallel energies of violence: Napoleon's battalions marching in; English guns bombarding them; the rumble of gunfire in the hills in the first world war; bombing and unspeakable cruelties in the second; the triumphant *bersaglieri* spilling off *Audace;* Tito's savage partisans flooding into the suburbs; New Zealanders riding their war-battered tanks past the railway station; the riots of the 1950s and the battles of the old Yugoslavia in the 1990s, which never reached Trieste but were fought not so far over its horizons. And the bora itself is like a blast of war: if maps were still symbolically ornamented it would be represented by a thug in a camouflage suit, toting a Kalashnikov.

THE PERMANENT element of dissent in Trieste, though, its immovable reminder of an alternative world of strangeness, harsh challenge, mystery and unconvention, where strolling instrumentalists may whistle the days away and the fearful excitements of battle are ingrained in men's memories—the city's real zone of disorder is the Karst. It is not disorderly in any criminal sense, no longer the haunt of highwaymen, by no means a desert nowadays, but even now it remains an antithesis of civic normality. Karstic landscapes in a generic sense extend far beyond Trieste, but the Karst proper, the limestone plateau over the sea which first gave its name to a geological category and an adjective to go with it, is mostly within the province of Trieste. Its presence is part of the civic consciousness, the origin of its melancholy perhaps, for before the Illyrians, before the Romans, before the Austrians or the Italians, the arid rocky Karst was always there—brooding sea on one side, frowning Karst on the other. Even now you can see the plateau from the very heart of the city, and in particular a great quarrying gash in its flank which always suggests to me a scar of surgery. Trieste cannot escape the Karst, and no other city I know is so obsessed with *stones.*

When I was small I was always excited by the Mendip Hills in Somerset, in whose lee my maternal forebears lived. They seemed to me hills of queerness, tantalizing hills, more disturbing by far than the stately old mountains of Wales that sheltered my father's people. I thought of them as mysterious places, and I imagined wild beasts and hermits up there. I have only lately realized that they too are karstic highlands, made of limestone and riddled by just the same caves and fissures as riddle the plateau above Trieste. The underground river Timava that flows into the Adriatic out of the Karst is attended by many a myth and legend—"vast with a murmur of mountains," Virgil called it; the river Axe that flows from the Mendips into the Bristol Channel is probably the original of Coleridge's sacred river Alph, emerging "Through caverns measureless to man/down to a sunless sea." The uneasy allure of the Mendips always made me think of outlaw lives, lives on the fringe, and perhaps it was a geological effect, because almost a lifetime later I am given a similar frisson by the presence of the Karst. Maybe Richard Burton felt the same, when he retreated from the Consulate with its flags, rules and dockets to his high study at Opicina.

Actually Opicina today is no more than a suburb, and Trieste's Karst as a whole is patterned by roads and by the big autostrada which sweeps across from Italy towards the Balkans. Many a commuter drives down to the city every day, or takes the funicular-tram. The boulevard along the ridge that nineteenth-century weekenders loved to walk is more popular than ever now: it is called the Via Napoleonica because it is thought the French made it for military purposes, but now it makes a perfect Sunday morning jog, with a pause to admire the seaviews occasionally, or a rest on a bench, and a cool drink or a coffee awaiting you at the other end. Bird-watchers, ramblers, collectors of mushrooms or wild asparagus, all use the Karst as a kind of park. I was at a children's party once at the extreme eastern end of the plateau, the very last protrusion of Italy into the world of the Slavs, and the families who brought their children along in their shiny Fiats and four-wheel-drives seemed to me just like enthusiastic supporters of a Parent-Teacher Association in some well-heeled suburb of the American Middle West.

Yet within the cramped confines of this territory—some twenty miles long, never more than eight miles wide—there are still haunting suggestions of stranger things. For a start there is the fact that closely all around lies a foreign country. There are six border crossings into Slovenia, and they still retain, for me at least, the old fascination of a frontier. I have always loved the moments of travel when, brought to a halt by a striped barrier, approached by unfamiliar uniforms, you feel yourself on the brink of somewhere unknown and possibly perilous. How expressionlessly that policeman waits, as you fumble for your passport! How uncomfortable is the silence, as he looks at its picture, then at you, then at the picture again! Do they put those sniffer dogs in everyone's car, or has somebody tipped them off that you are carrying cannabis? Will they find those uncomplimentary things you have written about their republic, in the manuscript in the boot? Is your visa out of order? Are you on a blacklist?

Nothing like that happens any more, when you drive out of Trieste into Slovenia, and all around the frontier posts today are welcoming bazaars of exchange booths, souvenir shops and cafés. Not so long ago, though, when Communism was in power over there, it could still be a darker experience. I remember approaching the border one Sunday evening on my way down to Montenegro. In those days of the Cold War, when Tito's relatively relaxed Communist Yugoslavia allowed a chink through the Iron Curtain, hundreds of Istrian Italians came to Trieste at weekends to shop or visit relatives; when it was time for them to go home again their cars approached the frontier in long slow queues, engines throbbing, sometimes lurching a few feet forward, sometimes subsiding into silence, waiting in the gathering dark to run the gauntlet of the security guards and the customs officers of the Socialist Federal Republic. The

Karst was dim and empty all around us that evening; when I looked behind I could see the lights of waiting cars bumper to bumper up the hill from the city.

The Istrians were used to it. Somebody had set up a mobile canteen, and they were selling coffee and hamburgers from the back of a pick-up. Once a pair of gigantic trucks jumped the queue by sheer bulk, forcing their way to the front of the waiting line yard by juddering yard until, with a hissing of airbrakes and roar of engines, they triumphantly disappeared. At last I reached the frontier post myself. Its lights were dim. An official with a red star on his cap beckoned for my passport without a word, and slowly examined every page. Without a smile, without a flicker, only a gloomy stare he handed it back to me. "Cheer up," I said. "Enjoy yourself," he morosely replied, and waved me through.

IN THOSE days this narrow countryside seemed to me instinct with subterfuge. As a lifelong aspirant anarchist I have always been attracted by the idea of a life of crime (feebly sublimating the instinct by taking face flannels from expensive hotels, to use as handkerchiefs), and there were taverns of the Karst then where the fancy seemed exhilaratingly real. How enjoyable to sit in some tumbled courtyard, high on the flinty plateau, eating home-cured ham and drinking chilled wine from the vineyard next door, while planning if only in the imagination escapades of bloodless villainy—smuggling spirits out of Bosnia, say, or robbing the downtown Banca d'Italia! How piquant to spend an evening in a crowded noisy inn somewhere near that froward frontier, trellised, trestle-tabled, jam-packed, with waiters dashing madly in all directions and jolly groups of friends drinking beer, and thinking that all around me conspiracies might be flourishing or double agents practising their deceptions!

Today the excitement has gone, and there are no sinister delays at the borders. Even so, sometimes I feel a tremor of the undercover still. Only the other day I stopped for an early breakfast at a café a mile or two from one of the frontier crossings, and there I got into conversation with a Dutch lorry-driver. He told me he had been delivering a load of tomatoes in Zagreb, and was on his way back to Amsterdam. It was his own truck, he said. He drove it all over eastern Europe, delivering one thing and another, picking up this and that for transport to the west. He seemed relieved to be over the border, though, and even as he mentioned the random nature of his commerce, I wondered if he had Chinese, Turks or indigent Romanys hidden silent in his trailer as he drank his coffee and prepared to move on.

EVIL memories of war linger in the Karst. Romans and Turks fought in their time up here, and there were terrible confrontations between Italians and Austrians in the first world war—down by the coast, the Wolves of Tuscany, two snarling animals of bronze, represent one of their most famous battles, when two unconquerable Italian battalions defied the worst the Austrian army could do to them. Many a village war memorial—very likely no more than a chunk of pocked and pitted limestone—remembers the men of these parts who fought with Tito's partisans, and near Basovizza, only a mile or two from the Slovenian frontier, there is a horrible reminder that in the wars of the Karst, as in all others, many victims get no memorial at all.

It is a creepy kind of *memento mori*. It is a pot-hole, one of those sudden natural pits in the limestone which are as common in the Mendips as they are here. It was excavated in the 1970s, and on a big stone nearby are inscribed the archaeologists' findings. At the bottom of the pit they found guns and equipment thrown there by the Austrians after their defeat in 1918. Near the top they found miscellaneous munitions from the second world war, together with the junk and rubbish that is thrown into holes anywhere. But half-way down the pit there was something horrible: a tangled mass of human corpses, male and female, some roped together. We are told that they were Italian opponents of Yugoslav Tito, both soldiers and civilians, some of them shackled while still living to the dead.

Whoever they were, they are not forgotten now. The hole has been stoppered with a big slab, and memorial stones are dotted around, as in one of the lesser battlefields of the American Civil War. The surrounding grassland is a popular place for picnics. When I was there one day a class of schoolboys was practising the skills of orienteering, and groups of them kept emerging from nearby thickets scratching their heads, arguing and anxiously consulting their maps. Two of their teachers sat reading in the shade of a tree near the pot-hole, and I asked them what the Italian word *salme* meant—I had read it on the slab, and didn't recognize it. "Corpses," they told me, "dead bodies"; and they looked at me with a touch of disappointment, I thought, as though I might have used my brains and guessed that for myself. And so I might.

On the lip of the Karst escarpment, gloriously overlooking the city and the sea, there is a monument designed to thank God that it is all over now. The huge concrete temple dedicated to Mary, Mother and Queen, was erected there in 1967 in votive thanksgiving for the end of the second world war, which had killed so many Trieste soldiers, murdered so many Trieste Jews, and thrown so many poor souls down the pot-hole of Basovizza. It is not a delicate structure, but it stands there cleanly and boldly, white against the sky, rather like, on a gigantic scale, one of those bathroom devices that disinfect the atmosphere.

THE KARST will always be a strange place. They may build roads all over it, they may suburbanize it or even industralize it in parts, but it remains an elemental slab above the city. Even now, between the developments, it feels like Slavic peasant country. It is a place of stones—drystone walls, villages of stone, churches of stone, stone houses, boulders and quarries everywhere—but with patches of extreme fertility. There vineyards flourish, and sometimes you may see leafed branches attached to gates. This tells you that the house inside is an *osmizza,* where wine and food are available. It is a sign inherited from Austro-Hungarian legalism—*osem* means "eight" in Slovene, and only for eight days in the year were such establishments licensed for business under *K u K.* In Grinzing or Sievering, outside Vienna, the leafed branch welcomes you nowadays to the decorous hospitality of tourism. Here on the Karst it is likely to be tougher stuff, and the people who serve you will be stocky, straightforward Slovenes with no pretensions. If it is a full-blown restaurant its victuals will be robust: goat, quail, wild boar, stringy prosciutto, sturdy pastas, nourishing soups, rough bread and fresh white wine. Noisy parties celebrate birthdays or graduation days. Landlords stride around the tables like amiable sergeant-majors.

These people have been hardened by history and by climate, but they have been moulded by geology too—it is a population perfectly attuned to its landscape. The Karst is not all forbidding. It can be welcoming too, a place of butterflies, lizards and cats in the shrubbery. In some of its pot-holes pigeons live, and one can see them lurking in the shadows down there, suddenly flying around for a moment or two, or reproachfully flapping their wings. Others have been filled with water down the ages, and are hidden away in glades of oak or ash, perfectly circular and alive with fish and dragon-flies. Sometimes reeds wave languidly at their edges, and small golden carp swim through, or big green newts hang head-down from rush-stalks.

The best known of these water-holes is called the Percedo. It is near the ancient village of Rupingrande, and it lies in the deep middle of a wood, the sort of natural wonder American pioneers stumbled upon far in the forested west ("Here we are my friends, by God's good grace, here is where we'll settle, and we'll call it Gracepool"—a circumstance recorded in *The Story of Our Homes and Hearths,* published by the *Gracepool Weekly Advertiser* . . .). We can stumble upon the pool too, in the dappled half-light, all alone with waterlilies all over it: and if we arrive at the right season of the year, frogs will be constantly jumping in and out of its viscous water—plop, plop, plop, they go, and it is the only sound in the silence of the wood.

There are vast caves and tunnels under the Karst, deeper than any in Mendip, some of them among the deepest on earth. One of them, the Grotta Gigante, has been tamed and floodlit for the tourists. Others still lie deep and dark down there, and through these the river Timavo flows on its passage to the sea. It rises normally enough somewhere in Slovenia, suddenly plunges into a chasm near the hamlet of San Canziano, crosses the frontier underground and reappears twenty-four miles later just as it is about to enter the Adriatic below the plateau. This mysterious sequence has inspired many fancies, and my favourite one is this: that when the Argonauts completed their mission into Asia to find the Golden Fleece, they returned to Europe by sailing up the Danube and its tributaries into Slovenia, where they discovered a stream flowing in the direction of the Adriatic. It turned out to be the Timavo, and when it dived underground they went too, and so arrived on the shores of Trieste. It was Jason and the Argonauts, claimed the nineteenth-century historian Pietro Kandler in all seriousness, who first established a chain of communication between Trieste and the Black Sea.

The Timavo still reaches the daylight near a village called Aurisina, on the coast beneath the escarpment some eight miles north of the city, blinking as it were after its long passage through the Karst. The site of its emergence is close to the coastal highway to Trieste, a road littered with hotels and cafés, and it is all too easy to drive straight by without noticing it. But if you stop, park in a layby and walk down a flight of steps into the woods below, you will find it a magical place. Mythmakers, poets and cultists have thought so down the ages, variously portraying it as the haunt of an Aurisinean nymph (as in

Revoltella's statuary), or a gateway into Hell. There is a small Gothic church down there among the trees, no doubt descended from a sanctuary of the pagans, and into the shadows nearby the river emerges in several channels out of the rock. It is a peculiar blue-green colour, and looks as though it ought to lie there thick and stagnant, but in fact it tumbles swiftly into the open, as though it is relieved to be out of the dark.

ANOTHER kind of arcanum survives at the other end of the Karst, in the village of San Dorligo del Valle on the Slovenian border. This is only two or three miles from Trieste's industrial zone on Muggia bay, but it is very Balkan. Slovene is generally talked there, road signs are bilingual, and the high ground nearby is slashed by a rocky ravine, the Val Rosandra, running towards the sea—harsh, grey, fox-haunted and raven-flown, with a solitary stone chapel perched hermit-like on its flank.

Here is the wonder of this place: if you go to the parish office there, and ask the priest politely, after apologetically rummaging about in a cupboard, with musty journals and account books falling haphazardly out, to be stuffed haphazardly back in again—"Forgive me, forgive me, I'll find it here somewhere, no, no, that's not it—forgive me—ah, this is the one, this is it"—eventually he extracts an ancient parish record kept down the generations in the Glagolitic script.

The Glagolitic script? The Glagolitic script. I have its alphabet before me now, in its two historical forms, and its letters are unfamiliar indeed. Some are rounded spindly squiggles, some are angular. All have a numerical value too, and they are strangely transliterated. "AZ'b," "Buky," "Vědě," begins the

Glagolitic alphabet, and its final letter is "Yžica." The script is said to have been invented by two Byzantine Christian missionaries, Cyril and Methodius, who came to these parts in the ninth century and found the inhabitants without a written language of their own. It was the first of all Slavic scripts, like no other European writing, and for centuries it defied the intrusion of the Latin alphabet. Its presence in the parish office of San Dorligo del Valle, so close to the city centre of Trieste, is like an unsuspected spell or exorcism, left in the attic.

THIRTEEN

The Biplane and the Steamer

It is also like a coded message out of Istria. In Istria the Glagolitic alphabet long ago became a symbol of Slavness, a defiant declaration, defying both political and ecclesiastical disapproval through conquest and conflict, assimilation and oppression. It was still alive at the start of the twentieth century. The peninsula was Triestine territory until the second world war, and just as that one strange document is stored in the parish vestry at San Dorligo, so Istria is always in the city's consciousness, still there in sight as in mind. The hundreds of refugee Italian families who came to the city when the Communist Yugoslavs took over Istria still form a tightly organized and influential community, resentful of the past and often fervently anti-Slav, and perhaps it is the loss of Istria, almost as much as the loss of purpose, that has given Trieste its sense of deprivation—a country so close, so familiar, yet now foreign territory!

I spent my childhood in Somerset, on the English side of the Bristol Channel, and Wales was my Istria. I could always see its mountains, so close across the water and yet apparently so unattainable. I knew it was my dead father's country, and so properly mine too. A lumbering old De Havilland biplane used to fly heavily over each morning on its way from Bristol to Cardiff, and its slow passing gave me my very first intimations of *hiraeth*.

ISTRIA is now almost entirely within Croatia, only a thin corridor running across it, just outside Trieste, to provide Slovenia with its outlet to the sea at Koper. It is a triangular wedge of land, about fifty miles long from north to south, never more than thirty miles wide, and its history has been labyrinthine. Its original inhabitants were apparently Illyrians. Its indigenous people now are all Croats or Slovenes, but it has been ruled in its time, in one part or another, by Romans, Byzantines, Franks, Venetians and Austrians. Bavarian Counts and Aquilean Patriarchs have lorded it there. Napoleon annexed it for his Illyrian Province. German armies occupied it. Yugoslav partisans fought all over it. It has been threatened in its time by Ostrogoths, Lombards, Genoese, impious Turks and sinister Uskoks from Senj. The Venetians built lovely towns all around its coast to sustain their command of the Adriatic, and one of them, Muggia, is now part of Trieste itself. Tito's Yugoslavia made most of the other islands into a People's Paradise, lapped by myriad hotels and camping sites. The eastern flank of the peninsula, the Cičen, was described by Baedeker in 1905 as "a bleak plain inhabited by poor charcoal-burners," and is now inhabited mainly by Romanians.

In Austro-Hungarian times, when the peninsula was under Trieste's jurisdiction, there were close sea-connections between the city and the former Venetian towns on the coast.

Capodistria, Pirano, Cittanova, Parenzo, Rovigno, all had, besides their familiar Italian campaniles, an Italian-speaking citizenry which thought of itself as part of a wider Trieste. Its business people came to Trieste to make deals or insurance arrangements, its ladies came to shop or go to the opera—imagine the demand for tickets, and the happy shipboard parties, when Smareglia's *Nozze Istriane* had its first performance at the Trieste Municipal Opera on March 28, 1895! Even in my own early days in Trieste, when the empire had long gone and a hostile Communist army occupied those ports, a small black steamboat belching smoke pushed off for Istria every morning. It reminded me of that old D.H. *Rapide,* on its way to Glamorgan.

The Austrians themselves created two Istrian coastal cities in their own kind, and both were familiar to Triestinis. When rich and loyal entrepreneurs of the Chamber of Commerce wanted a fashionable holiday, they took their families down the peninsula to the resort of Abbazia, which was a favourite of the Viennese aristocracy. It stood in the most beautiful situation imaginable, looking across the Gulf of Quarnero to the celestial isles and coasts of Dalmatia, and like Trieste itself it was more or less an invented town. In the 1840s it had been discovered as a winter health resort, and swiftly developed with hotels, gardens and villas. The most expensive Viennese doctors recommended it; the lordliest Austrian valetudinarians, the swankiest Hungarian socialites, the wealthiest Triestini speculators took their advice; in its late-nineteenth-century prime Abbazia was almost as smart as Nice or Monte Carlo.

It is still delightfully evocative of *K und K.* Some of the old hotels still thrive, curled and preposterously grand beside the sea; and on the hills behind, many a comfortable villa writhes with putti and dolphins, among gardens sentimentally fragrant with jasmine and magnolia. Franz Joseph himself often came here, and put up his mistress in neighbouring accommodation; a promenade along the seafront is named for him, and she is not forgotten either, for all the guide-books mention her. Abbazia is much modernized now, with the usual noise and concrete, but still Austrians come here by the thousand, together with a few Triestini, and it is easy to imagine flowered hats and epaulettes strolling the Promenade Franz Joseph in the evenings. (Did Franz Lehár conduct for them here, too? Perhaps, because for a time he directed a naval band in Istria, and in 1908 he published a piano arrangement of *Nozze Istriane* . . .) Just occasionally to this day one still meets aged relicts of the old regime, last representatives of the Habsburg patriciate, who incline their heads graciously when one meets them in the Botanical Garden, or bow in a courtly manner from the waist.

The other Austrian city of Istria was Pola, at the southern tip of the peninsula. This was very old, had been a Roman naval base, and was celebrated for its splendidly preserved Roman amphitheatre above the sea. It had a fine protected harbour, and when in 1856 the Austrian naval command decided that Trieste was unsuitable as a war-base, the fleet moved its headquarters here. The developers fell upon the town at once, to make of it a smaller, more martial replica of Trieste itself. Franz Joseph journeyed down to lay the foundation stone of its Arsenal, and all around it arose the familiar streets and buildings of an imperial town. There were the barracks, there the shipyards, the grand hotel for important visitors, the naval church, the offices of the bureaucracy, the club, the railway station for the track to Trieste. It gives me an odd sensation even now, for it is still like a miniature, shabbier version of that greater seaport up the line.

Where the citadel is in Trieste, so the citadel is in Pola. Where the offices of the Maritime Government used to be in Trieste, the Admiralty building still stands in Pola. The Riviera Hotel in Pola is like a poor relative of the Albergo Savoia Excelsior in Trieste, and there is a Caffè degli Specchi here too. And the lingering melancholy of Trieste is more potent still in Pola. The railway station down on the waterfront no longer sends its steam trains up to Trieste, only diesel railcars to Buzet, forty miles up the peninsula, and it is a bleak, forlorn cluster of buildings beside the tracks. Joyce, who lived here for a few weeks, likened Pola to Siberia, but this sad station, on waste ground beside the sea, suggests to me a final depôt on some remote South American coast, where the trains make their last stop before returning with relief to civilization.

Like as they were to each other, the two ports had diametrically opposite purposes. Trieste was a great trading port, dependent upon peace for its prosperity. Pola was dedicated to war. The most pompous buildings of the one were banks and insurance offices; the palaces of the other were structures of militarism. Comfortable passenger liners dominated the Trieste quaysides; grim warships were lined up, stern-to-shore, in the harbour of Pola. Trieste had an opera house. Pola had a Navy Band, with 180 musicians.

Still, their fortunes were always linked, to the very end of the Austro-Hungarian Empire. In Trieste the end was to be remembered always by the arrival of the *Audace* at the waterfront. It was marked in Pola, in the last week of the first world war, by the exploit of two Italian frogmen who penetrated the harbour's powerful defences and sank the battleship *Viribus Unitis.* She was the ship that had brought the Archduke Ferdinand's body home from Sarajevo to Trieste, and she had been built there six years before.

ISTRIA'S heartland, though, high in its karstic hills, remains to this day a purely Croatian territory of recondite fascination. It is the only place in the world where I have seen lightning going upwards from the ground.

This is what you must do when you arrive at the minute village of Draguć, far from the sea in the limestone uplands. Leave your car at the entrance of the village, which only has one narrow street, and walk between its old terraced houses to the small piazza beyond. The whole village is likely to seem utterly deserted, with not a sign of life, but if you cry a shout of assistance into the silence, four or five doors will open and four or five old ladies will simultaneously tell you where to find the key to the church of San Rocco (since they are all old enough to have been educated under an Italian education system, they will tell you in Italian). "Number Twenty-four," they will say, and sure enough there at its door you will find a sixth old lady already holding out a venerable iron key to you. Up to the very end of the village you must go then, and where it peters out into muddy rutted farm tracks, there all alone is the little church. A bit of a struggle with its antique lock, a loud creak as the door opens, and before you is a glorious Istrian surprise. About twenty feet long and empty of pews, the church is covered all over, ceiling and all, with wonderfully lively frescoes. They are naïve representations of the Christian story, a Bible in bright colour, and they were painted by an Istrian master some time in the sixteenth century. They are a masterpiece of Glagoliticism.

For here, although we are never more than a morning's drive from Trieste, we are in the heartland of that esoteric abstraction. It is a hard country, like the Karst, and its villages are mostly built on ridges or hilltops, and surrounded by walls to keep out the Turks or the Uskoks—even little Draguć stands there cap-à-pie. They are scattered and often deserted, sometimes abandoned altogether. They feel closely knit, though, perhaps because you can frequently see one from another, on a neighbouring high ridge across a valley, even when no road connects them; or perhaps because from their small taverns, as a mealtime approaches, an identical smell of stew follows the traveller from Roč to Vhr, from Cerovlje to Sovinsko Polje and down to Hum. Among them all, too, is a shared sense of inherited defiance, and this is because they were for so many centuries the inner keep of the Croatian culture, and of its ancient script. One can sense the presence of Glagoliticism always in these hills, a wistful wraith-like substance still drifting across the stony landscape.

The most celebrated of all the villages is a very depository of the tradition. You are led to it by a series of modern monuments, all in honour of Glagoliticism, its values and its heroes, forming an esoteric sacred avenue through the fields: a half-circle of stone chairs beneath an oak tree, to remember the teachings of Liment—a stone circle commemorating the Book of Istrian Law—a column in the shape of the Glagolitic letter

"Slovo"—a stone block in memory of Bishop Grgur—the Pillar of the Čakav Parliament—the Resting Place of Žakan Juraj—until, dazed or inspired by these queer mementos, you arrive before the gates of Hum, where a Glagolitic inscription offers you a welcome if you are friendly, a severe injunction if you are not.

Once a complete and prosperous medieval municipality, Hum is now a mostly empty tumble of grey stone houses, many of them derelict, within the minuscule circuit of its walls. It proclaims itself the Smallest Town in the World, and it is the true capital of Glagoliticism. In the tavern near its gate you may buy a postcard of the script, in one of the better-preserved houses there is a museum of it, and in the cemetery chapel outside the walls you may see a graffito written in it: a priest scrawled this in the twelfth century, it seems, as a reminder that Martin the Blacksmith was entitled to have thirty masses said for the salvation of his soul, and still had one to come.

When I wandered around Hum one dark and blustery morning I met nobody at all. Not a soul was around. A cock repeatedly crowed, a dog barked somewhere out of sight, but every house seemed locked and empty, and the wind blew cruelly through the dilapidations. Faintly, from some inmost hovel of the little place, I heard a telephone ringing. It rang and rang and rang, while the wind blew and the dog barked, but nobody answered it, and by teatime I was back in Trieste.

IN THE summer season a hydrofoil goes down the Istrian coast from Trieste, but it is no longer an organic connection. It is just for tourists. Today the peninsula looks more often eastwards towards Zagreb, capital of Croatia, or south to its companion holiday coast of Dalmatia. Few ladies of Parenzo come to the opera in the city nowadays, and only in the minds of those ageing refugees, forever brooding over their lost patrimony, is Istria still part of a Greater Trieste. Even the names of the peninsula have foresworn all Trieste affinities. Today Abbazia is Opatija, Pola is Pula, Pirano is Piran, Rovigno is Rovinj, Parenzo is Poreč, Cittanova is Novigrad, Capodistria is Koper, the Gulf of Quarnero is Kvarner bay. Istria itself is Istra now, and that little black steamer never sails away, trailing its black smoke, from the Molo Bersaglieri towards the blue-green shore in the south.

FOURTEEN

What's It For?

The fundamental fact about modern Trieste, underlying all that happens there, is that it was built *ad hoc*—to be the principal port of a continental empire. Ever since that purpose was lost the city has been trying to find substitute functions for itself, and for most of the years I have known the place it has been more or less stagnant.

A great city that has lost its purpose is like a specialist in retirement. He potters around the house. He tinkers with this hobby or that. He reads a little, watches television for half an hour, does a bit of gardening, determines once more that he really will read *Midnight's Children,* get to know Beethoven's late sonatas or try for a last time to get to grips with rock. But he knows that the real energy of his life, the fascination of his calling that has driven him with so much satisfaction for so many years, is never going to be resumed. He no longer reads the technical journals, because they make him feel out-dated. He no longer goes to professional conventions. The world forgetting, by the world forgot! What's it all been for, he wonders? Sometimes he feels he is cracking up or fading out, and he avoids the newspaper obituaries because . . .

A city seldom thinks about its own demise. The end will almost certainly never happen suddenly, except by war or grand catastrophe, and it will probably never happen at all. Cairo may no longer be the Grand Cairo of the Caliphs, but it is a vital metropolis still. So is the Vienna of the Emperors, or the London of the Raj. But all these are multi-faceted places, with purposes at once economic, political, artistic and perhaps spiritual. The cities most vulnerable to time, like the men in retirement, are the specialist cities, and Trieste is one of those—one can see from a map its God-appointed purpose, for it stands there at the head of the Adriatic like a conduit through which the trade routes of central Europe reach the sea. I used to have one of those pictorial aerial maps of the Alps, painted from a viewpoint somewhere over Bavaria, I would think, and all those high white peaks, all those high valleys, the plains and roads and railways and rivers of half of Europe seem to be looking towards Trieste, at the bottom of the picture. If it were not a port Trieste would have been nothing much, and the sense that it *is* nothing much, now that its great days seem to be gone, is what has made it feel so wistfully unfulfilled. Trieste is not exactly rankled by its disappointments, as a surgeon might be embittered by unfair dismissal from his hospital, but for nearly a century it has been nagged by lost circumstance.

IT IS a place ancient in history, but not in presence. Its true roots lie not in Roman antiquity, as the irredentists and the Fascists loved to argue, but in the commercial enterprise of the Habsburgs and their cosmopolitan agents. Other cities of Christian Europe, not least in Italy, possess a mystic dignity that survives from spiritual certainties of long ago, and helps to make up for civic setbacks. Trieste lacks this reassurance. No inspiring tower or steeple dominates the rooftops of this quintessentially secular place, such as ennoble the mercantile impact of an Antwerp or a Riga. Joyce thought the city "nourished on the food of scepticism," but I think it is dullened by ecumenicism. The creators of modern Trieste deliberately fostered religious diversity in the port, anxious as they were to attract able immigrants from foreign countries and faiths. There are lots of churches in Trieste, but because it was developed as a multi-national polyglot seaport, Christianity has been more thinned down here than elsewhere, and distributed among many sects and rituals—Roman Catholic, Greek Orthodox, Serbian Orthodox, Anglican, Methodist, Armenian Catholic, Waldensian.

Some of these temples are assertive enough: the Roman Catholic church of San Antonio Taumaturgo, St. Antony the Wonder-Worker, which we have seen standing grandly at the head of the Canal Grande, or the big domed Serbian Orthodox church of San Spiridione nearby, or the twin-towered Greek Orthodox church of San Nicolo on the waterfront, or the Jesuit church of Santa Maggiore which majestically surveys from its hillside platform the city centre below.

More often, though, Trieste's holy places are unobtrusive. The Benedictine monastery on the flank of San Giusto has been active since the fourteenth century, but does not look like a monastery at all. The enchanting little twelfth-century church of San Silvestro, where the Waldensians worship, nestles shyly in the shadow of Santa Maggiore. A steepled neo-Gothic church belonging to the Lutheran Evangelicals is almost unnoticeable among the downtown banks and offices. A classically pedimented Anglican church is tucked away in a residential street, and is used mostly as a concert hall. The church of the Evangelical Methodists, although its address is very authoritatively No. 1 Scala dei Giganti, is in fact all but hidden among the gardens of its now defunct cemetery. The small towered church of the Armenian Mechitarists, which now holds its services in the German language, dreams away the years in a side-street off a side-street, shaded by trees and beloved by cats. Even the hilltop cathedral of San Giusto is a modest enough fane, made of three older churches knocked together, and overshadowed by the neighbouring citadel.

So no Church Triumphant stands proudly at the heart of this seaport, and no holy processions sway through its streets with barefoot penitents and towering holy statues. The only miracle-working image I know of in the city is a Madonna of the Flowers which used to stand in the garden of a trattoria, and which bled real blood when deliberately damaged in a ball game. It became the centre of a cult, housed in the private chapel of one of the thirteen patrician families; and when they demolished the chapel, at the foot of the Old City, the figure was given a small niche in the entrance of the new building that replaced it. There it is still, within the loveless purlieus of a Government office block, safe from the missiles of sacrilegious louts and supplied still with flowers and candles, but hardly reverenced, in my own observation, by today's passing citizenry. I stood beside it for half an hour one day, and no Triestini crossed themselves when they passed it, or paused for a moment's silent prayer. Most of them are apparently not the reverent kind. In 1913 a new fishmarket building went up on the central waterfront (it now houses the aquarium). It was imaginatively equipped with a watertower in the picturesque form of a campanile, and the people immediately dubbed it, in their dialect, Santa Maria del Guato—St. Mary of the Gudgeon.

OF COURSE there are places of true numen in Trieste. The parish office at San Dorligo del Valle is one, when the gentle priest tumbles those archives one after the other from their cupboards (although there never was a St. Dorligo—he is merely a corruption of the Slovenian word for a pot-hole). Winckelmann's Lapidary Garden is another, especially when the music of the cathedral organ sounds through its memorials of two thousand years. In the suburb of San Giovanni there is a little thirteenth-century church, dedicated to the saints Giovanni and Pelagio, standing near a spring in the flank of the Karst: this was the start of a Roman aqueduct which took water down to the city, and like many source-sanctuaries it still possesses an innocently mystic manner. And No. 1 The Giants' Staircase is a sublime little retreat of tranquillity, through its private gate, among its trees, in the very centre of the city.

There are a pair of municipal saints, too, whose memories add something ethereal to the city style. San Giusto of the cathedral was martyred for his faith in Roman times by being drowned in the bay of Trieste with a lead weight around his neck. In holy legend the weight was metamorphosed into a boulder, this being a city of stones, and the boulder was later stylized as a sort of melon. The other civic saint is San Sergio, a Roman soldier supposed to have been converted to Christianity while on duty here; his image appears in stone beside the cathedral door, subtly converted from a memorial to a Roman lady by the addition of a halo. Sergio was martyred far away in Syria, in the same year that Giusto was thrown into the sea, and at the moment of his execution his three-pronged iron halberd miraculously fell out of the sky into the piazza outside the cathedral of Trieste, to join Giusto's melon in the city's ancient iconography. It is now the civic emblem, prominent everywhere, and on a column outside the cathedral it is shown protruding from a round melonian ball.

The original halberd still exists, too, at least for the faithful. It used to be on the top of the cathedral tower, but was knocked down by lightning in 1421, and is now kept in the cathedral treasury. There it stands modestly in a niche in the reredos, surrounded by reliquaries and saintly images, and illuminated by the glitter of treasures below. Scholars say it is not in fact at all like a halberd of Roman times, being more probably a medieval Saracen weapon, and the only miraculous property it seems to possess is its imperviousness to rust. Be that as it may, once a year on the saint's feast day it is carried in procession through the cathedral, attended by vestmented priests and choirs. I happened upon this ceremony purely by chance one day, when I was helping to make a television film at San Giusto, and just for a moment, as the procession of priests and choristers passed shimmering through the dark building, incense-burners swinging, golden-clad canons of solemn movement, lovely chanting echoes from the high rafters, and on a silken cushion the refulgent halberd itself, fallen from the empyrean so many centuries before—just for once I felt in Trieste some of the transcendental mystery that gives more spiritual cities their resilience. It was only a transient epiphany, though, and next time I went to the cathedral the halberd was back in its niche again, and not shining at all.

There is one more remembrancer of Trieste which I have not seen, but which sounds genuinely holy. In the deep waters of Trieste bay, not far off Miramare, on the bottom of the sea stands a life-size figure of San Giusto—San Giusto del Mare. He is standing, I am told, four-square on the sea floor, bound, and holding not the melon of his tradition, but the original lead weight of his martyrdom. All around him fishes swim, and occasional pious skin-divers.

Post-Christian faiths have mostly passed Trieste by. In eastern Europe one bright light that shone among the dark delusions of the Stalinist years was the flame of true belief. Colours might be dimmed in Prague or Belgrade, shops might be bare, the totalitarian pall lay like a drab cloak over everyone's lives, but still there were people who honestly believed that the system was just, and the gleam in the eye of the believer had its own beauty. Trieste has never been ideologically inspired in this way. The imperial idea was at best a commercial convenience for this city. Irredentism was no more than nationalism. Fascism, popular though it was, seems to have been more a fashion than a conviction. The nearest I sense to public spirituality today is the enthusiasm of the young New Age enthusiasts of the place, whose consciousness-raising meetings, organic cookery demonstrations, natural healing demonstrations, yoga classes, aromatherapy sessions and Ritual Trance Dances do add a touch of the other-worldly to the civic ambiance.

No, from the start Trieste's true inspiration, which brought it fame, glory and satisfaction, was money, accumulated by hard work. Its one ideology was materialism, with the conservative principles that go with it. What was the worst moral failing? asked an "ethical drama" performed before His Excellency the Governor in 1786, and the answer was not Dishonesty, Lechery or Treacherous Inclinations, but Idleness. Trieste was the Philadelphia of Europe, wrote a Frenchman in 1807, whose pioneers worked steadily and with iron will "in the shade of the caduceus of Mercury and the trident of Neptune." Mercury and Neptune were to remain its presiding divinities ever afterwards, together with semi-sacred patrons like Progress, Commerce, Industry and Abundance. Wherever you look to this day emblems of wealth and diligence ornament rooftops or add a sober grandeur to streets. Security, Labour and Navigation stand guard in the old Lloyd Triestino offices. In the lobby of the headquarters of Riunione Adriatica di Securtà, one of the founding insurance companies of Trieste, two ravenous lions and a lioness are held in restraint by a helmeted hero whom I take to be Security, or perhaps Accountancy. What is the message of that Fountain of the Four Continents, which stands like a mound of stones in the Piazza Unità? Why, it tells us that the wealth of the world pours through Trieste to fill or buy those barrels and packing-cases at the top, and at its corners characters representing all four continents raise their products in tribute to the profitable civic genius.

In its great days Trieste must have seemed a marvellous mechanism. "A colossal emporium and a prodigious trading centre," Jules Verne called it in 1874, and the empire did everything it could to channel trade Via Trieste. Four railway lines conveyed the goods of the four continents in and out of Europe. One went by Ljubljana to Graz and Vienna; one via Udine to Salzburg, and thence to Munich; one via Gorizia to

Prague; one southward to Pola. The central station in those days was decorated with lavishly elevated frescoes of Success, and although the southern station has long been disused, it is still proud enough as a railway museum, a treasure-house of old photographs, timetables, telegraph machines, model trains, signalling maps, uniforms and half a dozen old locomotives, for ever rusting with their carriages on the tracks outside.

Complex manipulations of railway route and tariff kept the port competitive. The great threat to Trieste was the rise of the continental North Sea ports, Hamburg, Bremen, Rotterdam, and Amsterdam, which were almost as close as Trieste itself to the markets of the European interior. Sometimes the German railways stole a march by reducing rates on traffic to Hamburg, but one great advantage Trieste offered was an arrangement for combined tariffs—land transport, port dues and shipping costs all in one fee. If an exporter shipped via Trieste he could pay a single fare for his goods to go from Munich to Shanghai, say, and have done with it. Trieste became Europe's chief point of contact with the Orient, especially after the cutting of the Suez Canal: even the British, when they wanted to reach their Indian empire in a hurry, sent their mail and couriers across the continent by rail to Trieste, to pick up a Lloyd Adriatico packet to the east.

Naturally the docks themselves were always the point of Trieste. Everything looked towards the wharfs and quays, as the mountains themselves looked down there in that fanciful Alpine map of mine. It was above all a place of ships and sailors, and Maria Theresa herself had instituted a nautical school, to be run by Jesuits—its successor still exists, opposite the Civic Library. The Austrian East India Company had its base here, in the days when all European States were competing for markets in the east, and built ships in its own Trieste yards, not far from today's railway station.

If you drive through the industrial quarters beside Muggia bay, with docks and warehouses all around you, and elevated highways threading over and under one another, you may notice an apparent castle tower protruding diffidently out of the chaos—more like a cardboard tower than a real one, with a pair of lions prominently prancing beside it. This is the tower of the Lloyd Austriaco Arsenal, for generations the headquarters of shipbuilding in Trieste. Great ships were built in this city for a century or more, and names that were famous all over the world were born to a splash of champagne on Trieste slipways. Here the *Viribus Unitis* was built, and two other powerful dreadnoughts which represented Austro-Hungary's will to be a major naval power, but which, as it turned out, were the last Austrian battleships. It was at the Cantiere San Marco here that Mussolini laid the keel of the battleship *Roma,* one of the only class of battleships ordered by the Fascist regime, and as it happened the last ever to be built for the Italian Navy, too.

Most memorably of all, at Trieste between the wars was built one of the loveliest of all passenger liners, the *Conte di Savoia* (48,500 tons), which with her sister ship *Rex* for a few years of the 1930s made Italy stylishly supreme on the Atlantic shipping routes. I grew up with these great ships. I pored over their pictures in shipping magazines, thrilled to their graceful lines, and marvelled to imagine their elegant shapes, streaming smoke from their two funnels, swelling foam from their prows, as they made at twenty-eight knots for Sandy Hook—ships, names, places that spelt romance for me then, and excite me still. I used to fancy that it was *Rex* or *Conte di Savoia* that I saw through my telescope streaking up the Bristol Channel, instead of colliers plodding into Cardiff, or banana boats for Avonmouth!

They are gone, all those great vessels, gone with the old greatness of Trieste itself. They had sad ends. The *Viribus Unitis* was meanly sunk that day at Pola—meanly, because she had already been handed over by the defeated Austro-Hungarian Navy to the new Yugoslav Kingdom, a possible rival to Italian pretensions in the Adriatic. The *Roma* was vindictively sunk by a German glider bomb in 1943, when the Italians had already signed their armistice with the western allies, and she was on her way to surrender to the British. As to the two magnificent liners, I mourned them in death as I had admired them in life. *Conte de Savoia* I saw for myself at last, after so many years of fancy, sunk, scarred and rusty in shallow water off Venice. *Rex* was lying burnt-out on her side, like a rotting and scabrous whale, when for the first time in my life I looked out from Trieste towards the coast of Istria.

EVEN in its prime there were signs of the city's vulnerability. It was a one-purpose town, and seers recognized even then that it could easily be ruined. But it held on until the first world war. Until that catastrophe shippers the world over still preferred to send their goods Via Trieste, and the tall-funnelled steamers of Lloyd Austriaco were still to be seen basking on advertising posters, surrounded by sampans in exotic harbours, while passengers with parasols daintily disembarked. But the collapse of *K u K* meant that the city had lost its occupation. There was no money in its grand old banks: all their deposits had been removed to Vienna at the start of the war, and Milan's *Corriere della Sera* likened the city in 1919 to a millionaire who had lost his safe, and was left to languish in poverty.

Handed over to Italy, Trieste had no organic purpose. It was not needed. Venice, Naples and Genoa were all well-developed ports. Trieste's trade with central Europe calamitously declined, and it was like a last skewed demonstration of old functions when in 1920 shiploads of soldiers of the legendary Czech Legion arrived from Russia. Technically they were deserters from the old imperial army, but they were packed off in trains, like so many cargoes before them, into the heart of the disintegrated empire, where they were welcomed as patriotic heroes.

Only passenger traffic saved the port from ignominy, because from the quays beside the Piazza Unità liners did still sail across the world. Two 24,000-ton motorships of the Cosulich Line, *Vulcania* and *Saturnia,* maintained an Atlantic service, and the ships of Lloyd Triestino were busy too. Now many of their passengers were emigrants, and most of them were Jews. Thousands of disillusioned citizens of central Europe took passage to the United States of America, by the route that had so long been habitual to the old empire. Thousands more left the *shtetls* of Russia and Poland to look for their new Zion in Palestine. Those posters of sunburnt tourists in the east gave way to pictures of open-necked young pioneers making for the *kibbutzim,* beneath fiery slogans in Hebrew. Elderly vessels were mostly used for the trade, and they were like mirror images of those desperate old ferries one later saw being turned away from the beaches of Palestine: loaded not with despairing souls of exodus, but with emigrants full of hope. The business was profitable for Lloyd Triestino, which made its own direct arrangements with the Zionist movement, until the Fascist Government instructed the company "not to pay too much attention to the Jewish trade"; and Adolf Hitler doubtless watched with approval, for he had told the nations of the world that they were welcome to all the German Jews they liked, "even if they went there in luxurious ships . . ."

The Fascists, looking for purposes for their City of Redemption, hoped to make Trieste an exhibition of Italian modernity—like the Futurists, in their old dreams of fire, smoke and energy. For one thing they saw it as a centre of aviation. It had long been connected with flying. It was a military air base in the first world war, and several aircraft had been designed and built there. In 1926 a local company started operating flying-boats on regular services to Venice and Pola, with headquarters in a shed on the waterfront. In the 1930s this was replaced by a proper Maritime Air Station, boldly on the foreshore and conveniently near the Hôtel de la Ville. It still exists, converted now to other uses (Port Captain's office, Coastguard base, occasional concert venue) but still recognizably of its time and ideology—at its corners two very Fascist demi-torsos, male and female, strain themselves heroically towards *Cielo Nostrum*. I have in my hand now a modernistic catalogue cover from 1934 (Anno XII) which shows the Trieste waterfront as the Fascists liked to think of it. Stylized freighters line the piers before and behind; a sleek three-funnelled destroyer is at the

Molo Audace; either *Vulcania* or *Saturnia* lies stately at the ocean passenger terminal; and among them all there sweeps towards its white station, leaving a plume of spray behind it, a streamlined black seaplane.

Mussolini's Government also imagined Trieste as an imperial port once more. From here, they resolved, a re-born Italy would exert its power abroad. In 1935 the Italians invaded Ethiopia, intending to combine it with their existing colonies of Eritrea and Somaliland to create a great new empire in east Africa. Here was a purpose for which Trieste, "third entry to the Suez Canal," was better fitted than any other Italian port, and the Ministry of Public Works announced that the city had been "destined for imperial functions by the Duce." The port's own commissioner said Trieste would be the pivot of an undertaking that would "open up a new epoch in the history of national expansion, and in the colonial history of the world." Tanks, guns and aircraft became the port's chief commodity then, and its ships carried the pith-helmeted New Italians who were to colonize the new empire—"armed emigrants of the Dark Continent," the port commissioner called them.

Some of the rifles that were then sent to Africa, captured by the British a few years later, ended up as drill weapons for the Officers' Training Corps at my school in Britain. They seemed to me more like muskets than rifles, but I dare say some of them were presented in salute when Mussolini came to inspect the port in 1938. By then, although an invasion of Albania was still to come, it was really too late for imperial destiny. It was Anno XVI of the Fascist era, but before Anno XXI arrived the Italian empire was dissolved, Mussolini had been hanged from a lamppost and Trieste had lost its purpose once again. On the central waterfront at Trieste today, the chief reminders of those years are a liner terminal without liners, an air station without aircraft, the Saturnia rowing club and the Ristorante Vulcania.

THE NAZIS found no real use for Trieste. Their brief empire was doomed too, and it was their final annexation. When the Italians deserted them in 1943, and they declared Trieste an integral part of the Reich, they thought of it as a bulwark against the threat of Slav *üntermenschen* from the east—a last bastion of civilization, as Metternich had declared it long before. Their local newspaper, *Deutsche Adria Zeitung,* forecast that it would know splendid times again, revived by "the European idea," but in the event almost the only use the Germans found for the port was the transport of coal and bauxite up the coast from Istria. The British and Americans did no better either, during their period of governance. The British used Trieste as the terminal of the trans-continental route by which they transported troops to their own fading empire in the Middle East, but in general both Powers were more concerned about who Trieste should belong to than what it was for.

The place just struggled on, when once Trieste's post-war status was settled, and the Cold War of the 1970s and 1980s did briefly restore to the city some of its original functions. Eastern and western Europe were then divided into rigidly discrete blocs. The west boomed with capitalist progress, the east skulked in dogma. One country stood half-apart from this stagnant conflict: the Federation of Yugoslavia, which was ruled by Communists indeed, but had declared its emancipation from Stalin's Soviet Union, and which thus occupied an equivocal half-way position between east and west. Trading with the west, or even travelling there, was harshly regulated within the Soviet-dominated States, but people could go relatively easily into Yugoslavia. It became a sort of de-pressurising chamber, a rat-run through the Iron Curtain, and from Yugoslavia entrepreneurs could easily reach the easternmost outpost of the materialist civilization, Trieste.

The city responded, and became an international emporium once more. For some years it was a murky exchange for the commodities most coveted in the deprived societies of Hungary, Czechoslovakia, Bulgaria, Romania and Yugoslavia itself. Jeans, for example, were then almost a currency of their own, so terrific was the demand on the other side of the line, and the trestle tables of the Ponterosso market groaned with blue denims of dubious origin ("Jeans Best for Hammering, Pressing and Screwing," said a label I once noticed). There was a thriving traffic in everything profitably re-sellable, smuggleable or black-marketable—currencies, stamps, electronics, gold. Not far from the Ponterosso market was Darwil's, a five-story jeweller's famous among gold speculators throughout central Europe. Dazzling were its lights, deafening was its rock music, and through its blinding salons clutches of thick-set conspiratorial men muttered and wandered, inspecting lockets through eye-glasses, stashing away watches in suit-cases, or coldly watching the weighing of gold chains in infinitesimal scales.

After the fall of Communism in eastern Europe, but before the re-emergence of the market economy there, all this half-clandestine trade briefly mutated into a legitimate Balkan market, in the gardens opposite the railway station where Nora had waited for Jim. Thousands of Hungarians, Romanians, Bulgarians and Yugoslavs came in buses to shop there. They used to seem to me like looters of a despoiling army, except that in those early years of Europe's re-awakening they were shabby and diffident, were slung about with carrier bags, and were in search not of masterpieces, but of cooking utensils, anoraks, shoes, suitcases, toys and household gimmicks. The market had a gypsy air to it, and its wares were often picaresque. I was amused one morning to see a substantial housewife inspecting a line of sports luggage designed, so a sales leaflet said, "For Who Live Within One's Opinion For Our Own Adventure Instinct To Walk Around Metropolitan Jungle For Ever." What could such a slogan mean? I asked her. But she did not reply, perhaps because she only talked Ruthenian.

IN THE evening the shoppers boarded their dingy buses for the journey home. Every cranny, locker and cupboard was stuffed with acquisitions—packages dangled from roofs, boxes were stuck under seats, carrier bags were piled in the aisles and every child played with a bleeping space man. From the windows satisfied exhausted faces peered out through the cigarette smoke. I once buttonholed an elderly Hungarian, carefully writing a picture postcard as he waited to board his bus, and asked him how he had enjoyed his trip to Trieste. He said it was an experience of nostalgia—by which I prefer to think he meant, if only in folk-memory as it were, that it had been like an outing in the old times, when the zithers played on the lurching wagons and the peasant girls danced in their embroidered aprons.

But these encounters would soon be nostalgic for Trieste

too. Before long people could buy their electric kettles, T-shirts and remote-controlled computer games just as well in Sofia, Bucharest or Bratislava, and the emporium fizzled out again. The Balkan bazaar was no more, the garden opposite the railway station was re-developed, and all that remained was a respectable covered market like any other. Throughout the second half of the twentieth century nothing came to much in Trieste. One after the other, regimes and ideologies and changing circumstances had all failed to restore its old virility. It was as though that redundant specialist of mine, during a very, very long retirement, were now and then to try starting some new activity altogether, growing mushrooms or playing the stock exchange, only to find that his cellar was too warm for fungi, and the Dow Jones had collapsed around him.

FIFTEEN

After My Time

Anthropomorphising cities like this is generally a foolish practice, but so particularly fond and proud of their town are the citizens of Trieste that it often feels as though it really does possess a communal will of its own. At the start of the twenty-first century something remarkable happened to its spirit. It was as though it had been given a course of Viagra, and rediscovered its lost vigour at last—a civic virility that has come too late for me, and can only be fulfilled after my time.

What had happened? Perhaps it was Ricardo Illy's confident administration, which encouraged the city to look outwards once again, instead of permanently pondering its own disabilities. Perhaps it was the advent of a new Europe, which seemed to offer Trieste a revival of old opportunities. Perhaps it was the energizing spread of globalization. Perhaps it was a general feeling that Trieste could prosper best by being entirely itself, a city unique in geography as in history: "FUK NATIONS," said that graffito on the refuse bin, back on page 133, and perhaps the old place had reached the same conclusion for itself. Or perhaps, like a sheep farmer facing ruin in Wales, it simply realized in its civic heart that the only sensible alternative was diversification. It could no longer have one purpose: it must have many.

IT MAINTAINS its oldest functions. It is still a sort of capital, and four authorities have their seat here. A Prefect represents the sovereignty of Rome, like the empire's Governor long ago, and in the same palace. A Mayor runs the city from his offices below Michel and Japhez. One President heads the Provincial Government of Trieste, from his headquarters around the square from the General Post Office; another, established in the old Lloyd Triestino palace in the Piazza Unità, presides over the Autonomous Region of Friuli-Venezia Giulia.

Trieste is still an important great insurance centre, and of course it is still a port—no longer one of the world's great ports, but still the fifth port of the Mediterranean. Lloyd Triestino belongs to Taiwanese owners now, but a few of its container ships still sail from Trieste to places like Jeddah, Calcutta, Singapore, Hong Kong and Shanghai, which have known the house flag for generations: the successor to its palatial old headquarters of the Piazza Unità, the one with Mercury and Neptune on its balustrade, is a glittering glass palace almost overlooking its original Arsenal, the one with the cardboard tower and the lions. Most of the ships come and go from Muggia bay now, but the ferry from Greece still sails from the Molo Bersaglieri, and the Albanian ferry docks at the Old Port that Francis Joseph opened long ago. If there are no great liners or warships on the stocks of Trieste, there is generally a glittering cruise ship having a refit in the very same shipyards.

The port of Trieste still has a customs-free zone, last remnant of the Free Port that Charles VI decreed, and it has revived some old links with the European interior. A mile or two up the bay from the shipyards a long thin jetty protrudes into the sea, and moored at it are generally a couple of tankers. They are pumping oil ashore from the Middle East, as the freighters of the old Trieste unloaded their Egyptian cotton and their Damascene silks upon the piers around the promontory: and just as those old staples of the entrepôt found their way by road or railway over the Karst to central Europe, so the tankers' oil travels by trans-alpine pipeline far into the European interior, to be turned into gasoline by refineries in Austria, in the Czech Republic or at Ingolstadt in the heart of Bavaria.

Another tradition of the port robustly survives, too. Down among the industrial clutter of the docks you may detect a magnificent smell in the air—only a hint to begin with, only a suggestion, until gradually a rich aroma presents itself which, sniffing like a bloodhound, you may trace to a particular installation somewhere around Pier 7. It is a classic fragrance of Trieste: the smell of coffee. It pervaded the streets of the city in its prime, in the days when coffee was kept in huge barrels outside every café, and this aromatic dock building is still Europe's No. 1 warehouse of the coffee trade. Coffee from around the world arrives here, and is distributed across all Europe—or processed by Signor Illy's people and sent back across the seas again.

TOURISM is the first alternative that suggests itself, when diversification is needed—even the Welsh farmer immediately thinks of caravan parks. Joyce liked the fact that Trieste was in no sense a tourist city, unlike Rome, which suggested to him a man making a living by exhibiting the corpse of his grandfather. Fortunately Trieste can never become one of your centres of mass tourism, crassly subjecting its true nature to the satisfaction of its visitors. It has no sandy beaches and few great sights: package tourists will always do better in Venice, or in the seaside resorts of Dalmatia. Nevertheless at the start of a new century Trieste is self-consciously sprucing itself up for visitors. Streets have been pedestrianized, piazzas resurfaced, roads re-aligned, museums modernized, tracks laid for a magnetic tram service. In the summer one outdoor festival succeeds the next—sand was especially brought in, in 2000, for the Beach City World Volley-Ball Tournament on the waterfront—and the nostalgic songs of Signor Lupi compete with the beat of rock groups from the hangar of the Maritime Air Station.

I once dropped in upon a meeting of tourist developers at Muggia, the Venetian port which is now part of Trieste province, and asked one of them what he thought they could do with the little place. "Do with it?" he cried. "Do with it? It is a Portofino waiting to be discovered!"—and he had a point, for it does have all the prerequisites, a picturesque harbour filled with boats, quaint backstreets, an exquisite piazza, a castle elegantly positioned on the hill above. I have twice given myself lunch at the Trattoria Risorto, by the harbour, and each time the Mayor of Muggia has been lunching there too, deep in discussion with business folk, and envisaging, I would guess, the Portofinization of his fief.

Then there is cultural tourism. With its university and its ever-enterprising publishers, Trieste has never been slow to capitalize upon its past. Books about itself come in a steady stream from its presses, to pile up on booksellers' tables and congest the shelves of my own library. There has always been Winckelmann, of course, and lately the shrewd Trieste publicists have realized the universal appeal of a lost monarchy. Now that the passions of Italianity have faded somewhat they are exploiting the Habsburgs for all they are worth. Miramare is the chief single tourist attraction of Trieste, and now it is supplemented by sundry Habsburgian allusions. Maximilian himself has been elevated almost to the status of a myth—"That was a gift from *Maximilian,*" I once heard a guide sanctimoniously telling a group in the cathedral, pointing to a chandelier as though it were a sacred relic. Much is made of imperial influences upon the Trieste cuisine, in tortes and strudels and a luncheon snack called the *rebechin,* involving things like pork, tripe, goulash, sausages and Prague ham. The operetta festival at the Teatro Verdi has become a decidedly imperial event: audiences rise to their feet not only for the Italian national anthem, but also for the Radetzky March. Sissy is back near the railway station, where the Balkan market was, postcards of the Father of his People are on sale in souvenir stalls, the old coffee-shops are promoted as Historic Cafés and Trieste's writers of the Habsburgian years are celebrated as they never were in the days when they had trouble finding publishers for their books.

In its dying years the Austro-Hungarian Empire found itself immortalized in a flowering of prose and poetry—often, rather like itself, essentially atmospheric or allusive, charged with wry and nebulous regret. It found its last laureates all over its territories, and three of the most celebrated wrote in this

Urbs Fidelissima beside the sea. Italo Svevo the Triestino ironically commemorated lives and love in an essentially commercial city; James Joyce the Irishman extrapolated his view of Trieste into a view of the world; Rainer Maria Rilke from Prague was inspired, on a day of the bora in 1912, to write the best-loved of modern elegies. All prosper greatly in Trieste now. Hundreds of people come to attend the university's annual Joyce School, or study at its Laboratorio Joyce. Hundreds more follow the Joyce Trail, the Svevo Trail or the Rilke Path, armed with maps and pamphlets provided by the tourist authority, and pursuing in fact as in fiction the memories of the three writers—from site to site, apartment to villa, Golden Key brothel to Stella Polaris café, bench outside the railway station to guest quarters above the sea (for Rilke stayed in the princely castle of Duino, along the coast).

TRIESTE is re-inventing itself as a centre of science. It is up on the Karst, says one of the splendidly glossy promotional brochures that are the literature of the new Trieste, "on these hills from which the most ancient inhabitants of these lands used to look out to sea, that the Trieste of the third millennium is being constructed." It is true that up there startling things have been happening. There is AREA, a great science park where scores of enterprising companies do research into the human papilloma virus or ligno-cellulose degradation processes! There is ELETTRA the Light Machine, which produces extra-penetrative X-rays! There is the Experimental Geophysics Laboratory, which monitors endogenous phenomena deep in the Grotta Gigante! But all over the city, too, a bewildering variety of scientific institutions has developed—a centre for theoretical physics, a neuroscience centre, a Centre for Advanced Research in Space Optics, a school for advanced physics studies.

Many of these organizations have international links. The World Organization for Women's Science, for instance, is based in Trieste, with a president from Swaziland and vice-presidents from Nigeria, Cuba, Egypt and India. The Third World Academy of Science is here too, and so is the directorate of the International Centre for Genetic Engineering, with scores of subscribing countries and, I am sorry to say, its own Animal House. The conference centre on the Molo Bersaglieri is frequented by learned societies from all over the world. Optimists believe all this heralds a new place for Trieste on the map—a new dimension for the city. Mayor Illy himself wrote a booklet describing Trieste as "A Gateway to the New Europe," and suggesting that the new Trieste can be "an effective point of reference for the entire European Union." As the countries of eastern Europe are integrated with the European countries, so the theory goes, Trieste will once more be a Mediterranean outlet for a vast continental entity, standing at the very junction of east and west. Transportation, finance, science, tourism—diversification, Illy said, should be "united by the common element of the city's international character" to create a harmonious and unified Trieste System.

IT WAS a dream, he said, but it seems to be a galvanizing dream. Trieste's first summer of the new century—my last summer in Trieste—was a season transformed. For the first time in my experience Trieste felt a young city, perhaps a hyper-active city. More bronzed young sunbathers than ever packed the promenade of Barcola, flat out, buttock to bosom, along the stony shore, and scullers in the bay cockily swapped badinage with the elderly anglers on the Molo Audace.

Every morning something new and startling greeted me, when I walked through the streets after breakfast. If it was not a World Power-Boat Championship it was an International Exhibition of Pens, if it was not the Via Dante being repaved it was the Museum Revoltella being re-modelled. Almost every day I found a new series of marquees being erected along the waterfront, or another temporary stage. Music sounded across the city far into the night. There were book fairs, and antique fairs, and a Sissy exhibition, and an exhibition of old gramophone records, and a veteran car parade, and a dance festival, and a medieval festival, and discos, and flea markets, and the Beach City World Volley-Ball Tournament, and rock groups playing wherever you looked. And as that first bright summer faded, and autumn crept in with its promise of boras and gloomy streets again, there was celebrated the Barcolana, one of the chief yachting festivals of Europe, and Trieste's one great living spectacle. The city prepared for it as a last fling of the season, and in a thoroughly nautical way. Every store displayed a maritime motif. Every hotel was full of yachtsmen. Another long parade of white marquees went up, offering every kind of seagoing accessory or gimmick, and outside the opera house the Association of Bakers set up a demonstration galley, where the bakers worked in full sight of everyone, and gave away free buns. Eighteen hundred yachts had assembled for the contest.

That October the ruffian wind of Trieste blew in early. The

trees were whipped by it, the sea was heavy, rain poured down and mists magnificently swirled. As the regatta assembled for the start, beyond Miramare, the central harbour came thrillingly to life with speedboats, inflatables and rescue craft. A big white Coastguard cutter stood ready at the Molo Bersaglieri. A helicopter came and went from the Molo Audace. Loudspeakers boomed across the waterfront. All day long crowds surged this way and that, and the myriad flags and pendants of the festival fluttered in angry parallel through the tempest. It was a scene of mighty animation. More boats battled against the wild sea that day than I had seen in my life before—perhaps more boats than *anyone* had seen, yachts of all sizes, yachts of all classes, their sails spread far over the water in the wind, the spray and the gathering darkness.

It was a grand foretaste, I thought, of vitalities to come—or an echo of vigours past. Yet even as I watched, the Trieste effect intervened, like a migraine that clouds the vision, and in my dreaming eye I saw the whole bay empty and brooding again, and the castle all alone out there, and the float never bobbing on that fisherman's line.

SIXTEEN

The Capital of Nowhere

For of course portents of twenty-first-century Trieste are irrelevant to the theme of this book. They are anachronistic to it—and to me. Seeing them is like seeing my own rejuvenation, resurrection even, and I record them only as a duty, because I love the old place and wish it well. Anyway I long ago conceived my own idea of this city's real purpose. I believe it stands above economics, or tourism, or science, or even the passage of ships—or if not above them, at least apart from them. It seems to me that if Trieste were ever impelled to advertise itself on road signs, like towns in France (*"Son Cathédral, Ses Grottes, Ses Langoustines"*), all it need say about itself is *"Sua Triestinità."* To my mind this is an existentialist sort of place, and its purpose is to be itself.

There are people everywhere who form a Fourth World, or a diaspora of their own. They are the lordly ones! They come in all colours. They can be Christians or Hindus or Muslims or Jews or pagans or atheists. They can be young or old, men or women, soldiers or pacifists, rich or poor. They may be patriots, but they are never chauvinists. They share with each other, across all the nations, common values of humour and understanding. When you are among them you know you will not be mocked or resented, because they will not care about your race, your faith, your sex or your nationality, and they suffer fools if not gladly, at least sympathetically. They laugh easily. They are easily grateful. They are never mean. They are not inhibited by fashion, public opinion or political correctness. They are exiles in their own communities, because they are always in a minority, but they form a mighty nation, if they only knew it. It is the nation of nowhere, and I have come to think that its natural capital is Trieste.

THE ELUSIVE flavour that I enjoy here is really only the flavour of true civility, evolved through long trial and error. I have tried to get the hang of many cities, during a lifetime writing about them, and I have reached the conclusion that a peculiar history and a precarious geographical situation have made Trieste as near to a *decent* city as you can find, at the start of the twenty-first century. Honesty is still the norm here, manners are generally courteous, bigotries are usually held in check, people are generally good to each other, at least on the surface. Joyce said he had never met such kindness as he did in Trieste. Mahler just thought its people "terribly nice."

So do I. I am only an outsider here, and my responses may be naïve, but I am constantly struck by the public empathy of this city, expressed in small everyday matters—a comradely wiggle of the fingers from one driver to the other, when the funicular engine is hitched on to the Opicina tram, or the smiles women offer to perfect strangers when they join the queue for postage stamps. Time and again in Trieste I have made some casual contact, told somebody the time, asked the way somewhere, to find the encounter develop into a conversation full of delight. A man once noticed I had an antique Baedeker in my hand (*The Mediterranean,* 1911), and stopping dead in his tracks, there in the street, he engaged me in warm dialogue about the particular pleasures of old guidebooks. I much admired the reception Triestini gave to a couple of Romany musicians from Slovakia, who turned up one day to play sultry music in Via San Lazzaro: as the citizens walked up to place their lire in the open violin cases they laughed, sang, jiggled their heads to the music or warmly thanked the players, and some looked as though they would like to break into gypsy dance themselves, if they were not a little afraid of making fools of themselves.

And the fondness of Trieste people for their city's innumerable half-feral cats always touches me. Old ladies emerge from their houses with scrunched-up bags of pasta, looking for favourite strays to feed. Outside the Trattoria Risorto in Muggia, while the Mayor took his victuals inside, I once counted eleven happy cats arriving with every sign of familiarity for their daily rations. On the Karst I discovered a little nest of cats, dappled and half-hidden by foliage, surrounded by the mess of spaghetti and fish-heads brought there every day by solicitous neighbours. In Trieste animals are rarely scared of humans, to my mind a sure sign of civic integrity, come wealth or poverty, fame or ignominy, empire or dictatorship or Autonomous Region.

COULD all this be the true meaning of nowhere—this half-real, half-wishful Utopia? Certainly I believe it is what Saunders Lewis had in mind, when he called the best sort of patriotism "a generous spirit of love." Only the other day I tripped on a pavement in the Piazza Unità and fell to the ground, spilling straw hat, books, tape recorder and camera all about me. I was not at all hurt, but to amuse my companion I lay there flat out amid the debris, eyes closed, arms spread. I had not allowed for the patriotic citizens of nowhere, who came rushing to my help in their dozens, preparing handkerchiefs to staunch the blood or bandage broken bones, and murmuring soft sighs of anxiety.

EPILOGUE

Across My Grave

As we used to say at the cinema, in the days of continuous programming, this is where we came in. The clock-hand moves. The angel has passed, and the talk resumes in slight embarrassment. "Well now, yes, mm, what were we saying? Care for another glass . . . ?"

Another explanation for the kind of sudden silence which began this book is that somebody is walking over one's grave. In my case it must be an angler casting a worm for sea-trout on an islet I own in the river Dwyfor, an all-but-island upon which my ashes will one day be scattered. The angler notion is as valid as the angel theory, when applied to the Trieste effect. I looked at this city in youth under the angelic influence; I am contemplating it now in old age like a poacher in the dusk. When I likened it to an allegory of limbo, back in my prologue, I might have added that it was the limbo of life itself.

Birth and death are the ultimate bookends, and between them a muddied narrative unfolds. In the course of it there crop up moments, experiences or places which in retrospect, rather like faces in an identification parade, we recognize as markers: the experience of first love, perhaps, a song or a book, the dread moment when we first needed spectacles, the impact of some particular corner of the world. Trieste fulfils such a function for me. When the angel flutters by I see myself sitting on that quayside bollard with my notebook in my hand, worrying out some meaning to my nineteen years of life: when the angler creeps his way through the shrubbery to Llyn Gwallt y Widdan, the Pool of the Witch's Slope, there I am again, a septuagenarian, looking for truths still on the very same waterfront. Jorge Luis Borges got it right, when he told of an artist setting out to portray the world, but discovering that his "patient labyrinth of lines framed the image of his own face": so it is with me, after a lifetime of describing the planet, and I look at Trieste now as I would look into a mirror.

> I was the world in which I walked, and what I saw
> Or heard or felt came not but from myself.

Much of this little book, then, has been self-description. I write of exiles in Trieste, but I have generally felt myself an exile too. For years I felt myself an exile from normality, and now I feel myself one of those exiles from time. The past is a foreign country, but so is old age, and as you enter it you feel you are treading unknown territory, leaving your own land behind. You've never been here before. The clothes people wear, the idioms they use, their pronunciation, their assumptions, tastes, humours, loyalties all become the more alien the older you get. The countryside changes. The policemen are children. Even hypochondria, the Trieste disease, is not what it was, for that interesting pain in the ear-lobe may not now be imaginary at all, but some obscure senile reality. This kind of exile can mean a new freedom, too, because most things don't matter as they used to. They way I look doesn't matter. The opinions I cherish are my business. The books I have written are no more than smudged graffiti on a wall, and I shall write no more of them. Money? Enough to live on. Critics? To hell with 'em. Kindness is what matters, all along, at any age—kindness, the ruling principle of nowhere!

My Trieste has been a place of transience, but dear God we are all transients, and sooner or later we all become out-of-date—or as another generation's jargon has it, pass our sell-by date. I know very well that my computer, my fax machine, my mobile telephone, my video, my CD player, my hi-fi and my 16-valve four-wheel-steer air-conditioned car will seem as quaint to my great-grandchildren as the brass-and-mahogany relics of Victorian technology do to me now. And if for so long Trieste has staggered through history from one disillusionment to another, sometimes there have been moments when I have perfectly understood the self-portrait called *Man Screaming* which Egon Schiele painted after his return from Trieste to Vienna, and it has dawned upon me what a nightmare hiatus we all pass through, on the way from birth to death. Surely the only logical response would be to stand on a bridge and scream? But no, self-deception sees us through.

For all its traditional sobriety Trieste is a hallucinatory city, where fantasy easily brushes fact, and a lot of what I have written about it has come from my own mind. I could have gone much further. Haven't you heard Haydn's Trieste Symphony, or read that famous passage of Conrad's about the Trieste longshoremen? Didn't Mann write part of *Buddenbrooks*, the ultimate novel of the bourgeoisie, during his stay at the Hôtel de la

Ville? Wasn't Bunin's most famous tale originally called *The Gentleman from Trieste?* Didn't Eichmann escape through Trieste, on his way to Argentina? Don't they say Lord Lucan has been spotted here, working in the aquarium? In Trieste anything *might* be true. I wrote a novel once about an entirely imaginary Levantine city, and found when I finished it that between every line Trieste was lurking. I wrote a book about the entire European continent in the years after the second world war, and lo, there at the centre of it all was Trieste.

Life ends with that Triestine *leit-motif* "No more, O never more," but it need not end unhappily. In death there is no exile, no *hiraeth,* and my own hazily agnostic conception of an afterlife is rather Triestine too: a blend of the genial and the melancholy, the bourgeois and the conspiratorial, the plush and the seedy, the backstreet and the cross-roads, the wild and the respectable, in a place where regrets, hopes and high memories merge. Citizens of nowhere, unite! Join me in Trieste, your capital, and together we will watch the sun go down on the Molo Audace, along with Casanova, Isabel Burton, Joyce and Svevo, melancholy Saba, a couple of cats, the Eagle of Trieste, the King of Westphalia, old Signora Revoltella in her wheelchair, Mahler and Freud and Lord Lucan and all the others who have loitered here before us—calculating profits, polishing phrases, memorizing Smareglia, eating spaghetti scraps, plotting revolution, denying truths, imagining loves or just watching the ships or the girls go by.

There are places that have meant more to me than Trieste. Wales is where my heart is. A lost England made me. I have had more delicious pleasures in Venice. Manhattan excites me more than Trieste ever could, and so does Sydney. But here more than anywhere I remember lost times, lost chances, lost friends, with the sweet tristesse that is onomatopoeic to the place. What became of that innocent young man I escorted to the brothel on page 138? Dead and gone, and all his horses too, from an English countryside that is no more. The friend who came with me to the schooner on page 83? Still sailing his yacht about the seas, loaded with rank and honour now, but no longer the lithe young bravo who clambered on board with the *prosecco* that evening. Otto, my natural Triestine, was stabbed to death in Arabia long ago. The woman who slept one dreadful night at the Risiera has gone to her peaceful rest at last. And the stranger I bumped into that day at the Savoia Excelsior? What swing doors is he passing through today, with what arthritic difficulty, and what tender lies is he telling now that he is old and grey?

As for me, when my clock moves on for the last time, the angel having returned to Heaven, the angler having packed it in for the night and gone to the pub, I shall happily haunt the two places that have most happily haunted me. Most of the after-time I shall be wandering with my beloved along the banks of the Dwyfor: but now and then you may find me in a boat below the walls of Miramar, watching the nightingales swarm.

Trefan Morys, 2001

Something I owe to the soil that grew—
More to the life that fed—
But most to Allah Who gave me two
Separate sides to my head

Rudyard Kipling

BOOKS BY JAN MORRIS

Coast to Coast 1956
Sultan in Oman 1957
The Market of Seleukia 1957
Coronation Everest 1958
South African Winter 1958
The Hashemite Kings 1959
Venice 1960
The Upstairs Donkey *(for children)* 1961
Cities *(essays)* 1963
The World Bank *(for the World Bank)* 1963
The Outriders *(political statement)* 1963
The Presence of Spain 1964
Oxford 1965
The Pax Britannica Trilogy 1968–1978
The Great Port *(for the Port of New York Authority)* 1969
Places *(essays)* 1972
Conundrum 1974
Travels *(essays)* 1976
The Oxford Book of Oxford *(ed.)* 1978
Destinations *(essays)* 1980
The Venetian Empire 1980
The Small Oxford Book of Wales *(ed.)* 1982
A Venetian Bestiary 1982

ABOUT THE AUTHOR

The Welsh writer Jan Morris, who is seventy-five this year, has written some forty books and says that this is the last. They have included several historical works about the rise and decline of the British Empire, six collections of travel essays, major studies of Europe, Wales, Spain, Venice, Oxford, Hong Kong and Manhattan, two capricious biographies, two autobiographical works and a couple of short novels. She is an honorary D. Litt of the University of Wales, a member of the Gorsedd of Bards of the Welsh National Eisteddfod, an honorary Fellow of the Royal Institute of British architects, a Fellow of the Royal Literary Society and a Commander of the Order of the British Empire. She lives in the top left-hand corner of Wales.

LSC NC 04.16.2024 #

The Spectacle of Empire 1982
Wales, The First Place *(with Paul Wakefield)* 1982
Stones of Empire *(with Simon Winchester)* 1983
The Matter of Wales 1984
Journeys *(essays)* 1984
Among the Cities *(essays)* 1985
Last Letters from Hav *(novel)* 1985
Scotland, The Place of Visions *(with Paul Wakefield)* 1986
Manhattan '45 1987
Hong Kong 1988
Pleasures of a Tangled Life 1989
Ireland, Your Only Place *(with Paul Wakefield)* 1990
Sydney 1992
O Canada! *(essays)* 1992
Locations *(essays)* 1992
Travels with Virginia Woolf *(ed.)* 1993
A Machynlleth Triad *(with Twm Morys)* 1994
Fisher's Face 1995
Fifty Years of Europe 1997
Lincoln 1999
Our First Leader *(Welsh fantasy)* 2000
Trieste and the Meaning of Nowhere 2001